INTRODUCTION

When I have just finished exploring a certain district and writing about it, I am tempted to make extravagant claims. The last one always seems like the best. To be honest, I didn't expect to find this bit of Cornwall very interesting, let alone attractive, and now that I know how wrong I was the risk of going "over the top" in recommending it to you is all the greater. Right, then: the coast between Pentewan and Par has probably never been picked out by any walkers of the South West Way as their favourite - and yet the cliff scenery on both sides of Black Head is dramatic and beautiful, and few small ports in Cornwall are more interesting than Pentewan, Charlestown and Par. Again, the St Austell area would be a poor choice for anyone in search of wild, rugged and lonely inland scenery - and yet you can easily feel far "away from it all" on some of the little-known paths within a mile or two of Polgooth or Trewoon or St Blazey - or St Austell itself. Indeed, Carn Grey, not much more than a mile from the edge of the town, *is* wild, rugged and usually lonely, and like several other places visited on the walks offers a panoramic view of a fascinating and unique district. For "china-clay country" is indeed unique, not only in Cornwall but in the world, and its beauty as well as its harshness has been captured in words by natives like A. L. Rowse, Jack Clemo and Alan M. Kent (whose new novel, *Clay*, I especially recommend) and visitors like James Turner, whose book *The Stone Peninsula* begins, "The sun was bursting off the tops of the white pyramids of china clay waste near St Austell. .... In the wind the whole range of white hills shivered with this light, silver, blue and gold, magenta when a cloud passed over the sea." Those pyramids, and the flat-topped mounds which are now becoming more common, form part of the backdrop to most of these walks. For reasons of safety I have avoided working pits, but three of the suggested routes explore areas containing disused china-clay works, many of which are slowly being reclaimed by nat~~~ ~~~ ~~~ ~~~ metal mines. One of the many surprises I had while researchi the St Austell area was once nearly as im china clay. Admittedly, some of the famou modern housing or modern industry, but remains are still there in plenty, many of trees and undergrowth.

GN00708642

Enough! I feel myself approaching the top the walks.

ACKNOWLEDGEMENTS

As usual I have relied on help from many sources. Above all I am grateful for the expert advice I have received from Kenneth Brown and Charles Thurlow, both of the Trevithick Society, regarding mines and the china-clay industry respectively. My thanks also go to Valerie Brokenshire for help with several walks in and around Tregrehan Mills, to the staff at the Wheal Martyn Museum for their friendly advice, to Brian Heather for information about a famous black horse, and especially to the management of English China Clays International for their sympathetic response to enquiries about access to several places in their ownership.

SOME MINING TERMS

This book is written with the interested general reader in mind, rather than those who have made a special study of mining in Cornwall. Although some explanations of technical terms are included in the main text, I think a brief glossary may prove helpful. Please bear in mind, however, that these are very simplified explanations: several of these words have formed the basis of lengthy articles and even whole books.

ADIT A drainage channel with its mouth or **PORTAL** in a valley or on a hillside or cliff face. In deep mines the water had to be raised by pumping to the level of the adit; this is why statistics often state the depth of a mine "below adit". Adits also often doubled as shafts by following the metal **LODE** (vein), and in some cases provided access for the miners.

BEAM ENGINE Thomas Newcomen of Dartmouth (1663-1729) was the first to develop a steam engine which could be used for pumping water up from the mines. The cylinder was placed vertically, and the piston was chained to one end of a massive wooden or cast iron beam or **BOB** (see the sketch on page 34), pivoted on a strong wall, known as the BOB WALL. The other end overhung the mine shaft and was attached by long rods to the pump at the bottom. In the 1770s James Watt and Matthew Boulton began manufacturing an improved version, and James Pickard modified beam engines to produce rotative motion, used mainly for the **WHIM** (winding) and driving the **STAMPS**. Early in the 19th century, great improvements were brought by the use of high-pressure steam; the research and inventions of Richard Trevithick (1771-1833) made an important contribution here, but many other engineers also played a significant part. The size of each engine was expressed in terms of the diameter of its cylinder: 45", 90", etc.

Killifreth Mine, near Chacewater, some time between 1893 and 1897. The left- and right-hand engine houses, on Hawke's and Old Sump shafts respectively, were for pumping, and the rocking beams of the engines can be seen projecting from the bob walls. In the middle is the whim engine house, set at right-angles to the other two, so that its bob wall is hidden in this picture. The rotating drum, which is visible, would be used for hoisting and lowering in both the shafts.

BUDDLE A device for concentrating ore by means of gravity. Early buddles were rectangular, but in the 19th century most were circular; water containing the ore which had been reduced to a fine powder in the stamps was fed into the buddle at the centre or the sides, and rotating brushes were used to ensure that the heaviest, metal-bearing particles settled closest to the inlet point.

BLOWING HOUSE The early form of smelting house, in which the furnace temperature was raised by bellows, usually operated by a waterwheel.

CALCINER (pronounced "cal-*sign*-er") A furnace in which ore was roasted in order to drive off impurities such as arsenic and sulphur. If the arsenic was wanted, the fumes were passed though a long, zigzag flue known as a **LAMBRETH** (labyrinth), from which the deposits were collected.

COUNT HOUSE The mine's office.

DRESSING FLOOR The area where the ore was prepared for smelting.

FLAT-RODS Wooden or iron rods which were used to transfer power from a steam engine or waterwheel to a remote location.

LEAT An artificial watercourse. Where a leat was carried in a raised trough it was known as a **LAUNDER**.

SETT "The ground granted to a company of adventurers" (C. C. James) (Adventurers were shareholders in a mining enterprise.) The word "sett" was also used for the granite blocks used to carry rails.

STAMPS Cornish Stamps machines were used to crush the small lumps of ore into material like sand in texture. Heavy timber or iron lifters with iron "heads" at the bottom were raised by cams on a rotating axle, and fell on the ore, fed into a box beneath. Small stamps were usually powered by waterwheels, as in the picture (taken from the Perran Foundry catalogue by courtesy of the Trevithick Society), and larger ones by steam engines.

STREAMING The normal method of winning tin before deep mining became possible. Tin washed down into valleys and buried under silt was exposed, originally by shovel and barrow; the tin-bearing gravel was then sorted and washed, and the waste material used to back-fill the excavated area. Nowadays, earth-movers and lorries do the work.

WHIM A machine for raising water, ore or other heavy materials from the mine. The earliest whims were operated by horses, which walked round and round turning a wooden drum or capstan around which was wound the cable attached to the "kibble" or bucket. Some horse-whims continued in use till the present century, but the whims in deep mines were driven by steam engines, and these were known as "fire whims".

WALK 1
COOMBE AND DOWGAS
Just over three miles

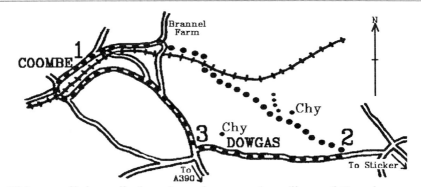

This easy little walk, based on the attractive village of Coombe, runs through an old tin-mining area on the southern edge of "china-clay country". Old shafts, overgrown burrows (mine dumps), several stacks and an engine house are on or close to the route. This is remote-feeling countryside whose peace is rarely disturbed except by the occasional train on the main London - Penzance line, which is close at hand during most of the walk. The paths and tracks used on the first half of the walk are likely to be muddy in places; the second half is on minor roads which seldom see much traffic. Most of the road walking is along a ridge which gives wide views, especially to the north. A couple of gates will probably have to be climbed. You may be able to get provisions at the post office in Coombe. There is no pub on the route, but a diversion would enable you to visit the Hewas Inn at Sticker, an attractive pub with an interesting and very reasonably-priced menu. This, however, would add at least a mile and a half of road walking, so you might prefer to call there with your car, as we did, when the walk had given us a good appetite.

Coombe is a mile or two south of St Stephen-in-Brannel. The easiest route to it is to leave the A390 St Austell - Truro road at Hewas Water, following the sign north to St Stephen and High Street. (I am writing this before the completion of the Sticker bypass; it seems unlikely that there will be access to this country road from that, so you will probably need to approach it from the old main road, running through Sticker and Hewas Water.) Coombe is signposted, but you may find it helpful to refer to a fairly large-scale map. If you enter the village by going under the railway bridge on the south-west side you will pass the post office almost immediately; then turn right, following the sign to High Street and Lanjeth, through the main part of the village, and if possible park beside the road somewhere before the first turning on the right, or not too far beyond it.

1 To start the walk, take that right turning, which runs gently uphill, still mostly among the trees that help to make Coombe (*) so attractive. Ignore

6

Landfall Walk Books No. 10

BOB ACTON

AROUND ST. AUSTELL

Black Head (Walks 6 and 8)

Circular Walks from Pentewan to Par

First published 1992 by
LANDFALL PUBLICATIONS
Landfall, Penpol, Devoran, Truro, Cornwall TR3 6NW
Telephone Truro (0872) 862581

A CIP catalogue record for this book is available from the British Library.

ISBN 1 873443 03 X

IMPORTANT NOTE

I have done my best to ensure that all the recommended routes are on public
rights of way, with a few unavoidable exceptions mentioned in the text, and
that they are all unobstructed. If you come across unexpected difficulties
(new fences, changed field-boundaries, rotted footbridges, waist-deep mud
....) please be patient, take the nearest practicable alternative route, and if
possible let me know about the problem so that I can refer to it in any future
edition of this book. Please help farmers and other landowners by leaving
all gates as you found them, and by keeping dogs on a lead when there are
livestock nearby.

USING THE BOOK

The boxed note at the start of each walk description is intended to be read
before you set out; sometimes it would be useful to make preparations a day
or two in advance in order to get the most out of the walk. A star (*)
indicates that there is a boxed note on this point - usually but not always on
the same page. The directions attempt to be very exact and explicit, but the
maps are only rough sketches, so I'd strongly recommend taking with you the
relevant Ordnance Survey maps. Landranger 204 (Truro, Falmouth &
surrounding area) covers most of the routes, but for the ones north of St
Austell you need No. 200 (Newquay, Bodmin & surrounding area). Best of
all for walkers is the Pathfinder series; the sheets named "St Austell and
Fowey", "St Newlyn East, Indian Queens & St Dennis" and "Mevagissey and
Tregony" are the relevant ones.

Typesetting, maps, drawings and photographs by Bob Acton

Printed by the Troutbeck Press
and bound by R. Booth Ltd., Antron Hill, Mabe, Penryn, Cornwall

---

COOMBE

Strictly, its name is St Stephen's Coombe, to distinguish it from the many other Coombes in Cornwall. (There are at least two within five miles of my own home - one on a creek of the Fal and another between Bissoe and Cusgarne - and both are beautiful spots, like this one.) Like the Welsh "cwm" it simply means "valley", or more accurately "small valley", in contrast to "glynn", "large valley".

---

the right turning, into a housing estate. When you reach a grassy triangle with a signpost left to High Street and Lanjeth and an unsigned road to the right, continue more-or-less straight ahead along a track which makes pleasant walking but may be muddy at times. The impressive farm buildings a little way off to the left are those of Brannel Farm, where quite a large area is devoted to rose growing. Brannel or Bernel was a Domesday manor, and the parish name includes that of its principal manor in order to distinguish it from the two other St Stephens in Cornwall, those "by Launceston" and "by Saltash". The manor house itself was at Court, a little further north than the farm. Close by on the right is the railway line, but it is on a higher level and you may not be aware of it unless a train passes. Soon, however, the track takes you under a railway bridge. Then turn left, still keeping near the line at first. On the skyline to your left now is the massive Blackpool china clay works. Ignore the bridge over the railway: go through the farm gate ahead (it has to be lifted), and walk up the rather muddy little lane between hedges which soon brings you to Lower Dowgas farm, complete with thatched farmhouse and two Shetland ponies. I'm not sure how permanent a feature the ponies are. Continue ahead along the obvious grassy lane, and soon you are passing among old shafts and waste-heaps, now mostly shrouded in thick vegetation - relics of St Austell Consols Mine (*). Ignore the right fork. Where the grassy track curves sharply to the right, go through the wooden farm gate on the left or over the stile near it, and turn right on the stony track. You should now be close to a tall chimney, and soon a side-track to

---

ST AUSTELL CONSOLS

This was made up of several small old mines, at least one of which (Wheal Unanimity) was at work in the 18th century; others were called Hawkins and Trewithen, and East Wheal Strawberry was formed in 1835. The group, together with part of Great Dowgas, became St Austell Consols in 1844, and in 1864 the depth of the workings reached nearly 500 ft. During the 1860s engine houses for pumping, winding and stamps were built. In 1873 another company, St Stephen's Tin and Copper Mines, took over parts of the sett, but this seems to have been short-lived. Hamilton Jenkin tells the story of "a Mr Bargett" who in about 1907 hunted for nickel in the waste-dumps of this mine and "stored his finds in a nearby shed. At a later date the shed was removed and its contents thrown back on the burrows whence many good specimens of the ore were subsequently recovered by mineral collectors." Apart from nickel, tin and copper, the mine has also produced some uranium and cobalt.

---

the left allows you to take a close look at it. It belonged to a beam engine used for driving the stamps at St Austell Consols. Close to the stack on the west a square depression in the ground marks the site of the boilerhouse. Still continue along the main track, among more mine workings, including a shaft on the left surrounded by a low wall. Somewhere near here, according to the OS Pathfinder map, the right of way diverges to the left from the main track, but we failed to find it, so unless it is reinstated at some future date walkers have no choice but to continue along the track - and that appears to be the right of way according to the Landranger map. Go through the wooden farm gate, then past an old building on the right, now in agricultural use but probably, in Kenneth Brown's opinion, originally the mine's smithy. The metal farm gate (padlocked when we did this walk) brings you to a road.

2 Turn right on that. *If, however, you want to include a visit to the Hewas Inn at Sticker on the walk, turn left and then take the second turning on the right. After about half a mile this brings you to the A390 just beside the pub.*

Great Dowgas Mine
On the skyline are the huge waste tips of Blackpool china clay pit.

Return the same way. This minor road runs almost due west, giving you good views to the right across the mining territory you have just walked through, to the distant china clay tips, with the village of Nanpean on the skyline. On the ridge to the left is the engine house of Ventonwyn mine (*), with its separate stack. Just beyond Dowgas House is another lone stack, this time belonging to the arsenic calciner of Great Dowgas Mine (*). An unusual feature of the chimney is that even the top part is built of stone: normally brick was used because it was more convenient for the tighter circle and thinner wall as the stack tapered.

GREAT DOWGAS MINE

The name, "Dowgas", is from the Cornish *dew cos,* two woods. There's not much woodland at Dowgas now, and perhaps the mines are largely responsible for that: huge quantities of timber were consumed by mining, especially in order to supply charcoal for smelting in blowing-houses. By 1719, however, Great Dowgas Mine was sending tin to the smelting house at Calenick, south of Truro, one of the earliest to use the new "reverberatory" furnaces, which burnt coal and anthracite instead of wood and charcoal. (See Walk 12 in *A Second View from Carn Marth.*) Like Polgooth Mine (Walk 5 in this book), Great Dowgas was fortunate in working lodes some of which were at shallow depths, and as at Polgooth much of the earlier mining was by means of an open cut. (The most famous example of this form of tin mining was at Carclaze, north of St Austell, whose impressive pit attracted many visitors. By 1850, according to one estimate over a million tons of ground had been excavated. There is a vivid description of it in George Henwood's *Cornwall's Mines and Miners* (c. 1857-9). It is now a china-clay works.) What Hamilton Jenkin calls "quarry-like excavations" on Goffan, Goffins or Great Stopes Lode at Dowgas were still clearly visible when he was writing *Mines and Miners of Cornwall* during the 1960s, but they were filled in about ten years ago. During the 19th century, deeper mining was carried out. Hamilton Jenkin tells the remarkable story of a group of six men who in 1828 took only six weeks to sink a shaft of 37 fathoms (222 ft.); their pay totalled £40, and for that they also excavated the plat and erected a horse-whim! (Sorry about the technical terms .... a plat was a flat area, in this case for the horse-whim, a capstan-like structure used for winding and turned by literal horse-power.) The same George Henwood I mentioned just now referred to the "Hot Lode" at Great Dowgas, saying it was one of the hottest in Cornwall: "the roof and sides of the workings are studded with minute crystals and efflorescence from the decomposing iron pyrites, the heat from which cause is so oppressive that a visit of a few minutes is all that can be safely endured." The mine continued to be worked for both tin and copper at various periods during the 19th century, and its last period of activity was from 1905 to 1913, in conjunction with Ventonwyn Mine. Details of this final working, together with four photographs which show how much has changed in 80 years, are in the 1985 issue of *The Journal of the Trevithick Society.*

3 At the crossroads turn right. Ahead now in the middle distance is the tower of St Stephen church, with a backdrop of china-clay tips. Either of the two right turnings would bring you back into Coombe, but to avoid covering again some of the ground you have already walked ignore those and continue on the "main" road as it curves downhill and then runs beside the railway line, finally passing under the bridge beside Coombe post office and chapel.

Another walk including Coombe is in Around Mevagissey. *The route also passes through Grampound and St Stephen, and is of special interest to anyone who would like to know more about the china stone industry.*

VENTONWYN MINE

The stamps engine house of Ventonwyn is among the best-known in the county, being a very dominant feature, especially to those driving towards St Austell on the A390; and it shares with several other famous ones such as Wheal Coates near St Agnes the dubious distinction of having been built for a comparatively unsuccessful mine. Originally called Wheal Elizabeth, it was, as Dines puts it, "worked in a small way for many years", but the only recorded output is of 138 tons of black tin between 1903 and 1907, which is when the stamps engine was used. The name, meaning "white spring" or possibly "beautiful spring", is that of a nearby farm.

(Continued from page 14)

mine is by means of ladders, placed almost perpendicularly: at the foot of each ladder is a narrow break, or landing-place; and at certain intervals, are openings into different beds of ore.

At about fifty or sixty feet below the surface of this mine, the water that percolates through the different strata begins to form small streams, which would soon increase, and overflow the lower part of the mine, if not constantly conveyed away. This process is performed by the stupendous steam-engine noticed above, which raises the water to the adit-level like the fountain of a river. The quantity of coals requisite to fill the fire-place beneath the boilers of this immense machine is sixty bushels; and the consumption every twenty-four hours is about three weigh and a half, or 144 bushels. The expences of erecting the engine were nearly 20,000*l.* The whole operation of the machine may be suspended by a slight pressure on a sort of bolt attached to a large valve. Borlase mentions that in his time the produce of this mine was so great, that the proprietors gained 20,000*l.* annually for several successive years. The revenues now obtained from it are very great: but it has not always been so productive. Once, about the year 1754, it stopped working, the receipts having exceeded the charges only ten pounds in the preceding ten years! though the expenditure during that time was 100,000*l.*

* " When a stranger is induced to descend, he is previously accoutred in a flannel shirt and trowsers, a close cap, an old hat to shelter his face from droppings, and a thick pair of shoes. A lighted candle is put into one hand, and a spare one suspended to a button of his jacket. Every part of the ordinary dress is laid aside, and the flannel dress worn close to the fkin, in order to absorb the profuse perspiration which the closeness of the mine, or the labor of mounting the ladders, may occasion."

* Maton's Observations on the Western Counties.

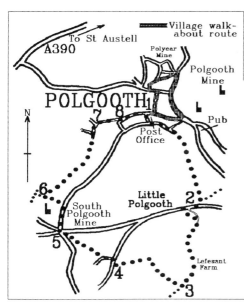

WALK 2
POLGOOTH
Under three miles

This is a pleasant short walk featuring attractive countryside along with plenty to interest the "industrial archaeology" enthusiast. The going is mostly easy, but mud is to be expected on at least one part of the route. Polgooth has a shop where you can buy provisions, and also a large, quite "up-market" pub well-known locally for good food. A short stroll round the village is suggested as a little "extra" in the note about Polgooth.

Polgooth is signposted from the A390 a couple of miles west of St Austell. The village streets are rather narrow, but roadside parking is usually possible near the post office. Alternatively you could, with permission, use the Polgooth Inn car park, though this tends to be full, especially at weekends.

1 From the post office / store at Polgooth (*), take the side road (past the post box), and at the Polgooth Institute turn left. You are now on Bal East Lane, a name which reflects the importance of mining to this village. On the hill ahead now, in the middle of the St Austell Golf Course, is Taylor's pumping-engine house, the most prominent relic of Polgooth Mine (*); and soon you get a view of another engine house, currently being very imaginatively converted into living accommodation, in the valley below. A narrower path down to the left (at the point where the track curves right) would bring you to the Polgooth Inn, if you're ready for that so soon. The main track is tree-lined and has good valley views: pleasant walking. After less than half a mile it brings you past a bungalow and down to a road a few yards beyond that. (Ignore the signed footpath going left.)

2 Turn right on the road, and then almost immediately left; use either the concreted road or the rough track on the right of it: they soon meet again. The minor road now goes uphill past Lefesant Farm and then becomes a rough track, passing a converted farm building.

3 Be careful not to miss the right turning that comes quite soon, where there are a few steps down and then a muddy patch followed by a steepish, narrow path that is evidently used by horses. ("Muddy Lane" is the locals' name for it, apparently, and when we were there, in the moist June of 1991, it was certainly sticky.) At the top you have a good view over St Austell, with huge china-clay dumps on the skyline. Continue ahead on a track, with

(Directions continue on page 14.)

11

POLGOOTH

The name probably means "goose pool", which perhaps implies a farming community, but for centuries life in the village was dominated by tin and copper mining (the latter mainly in the first half of last century). Nowadays its roles seem to be mainly as a dormitory for St Austell and towns as far away as Plymouth, a site for pleasant retirement homes, and a magnet for weekend visitors attracted by its very popular pub; but relics of the mining are by no means limited to the two ruined engine houses overlooking it from the east and the south-west. To see some of the others, I suggest a short stroll round part of the village not included on the main walk, as follows. From the post office go down Fore Street (i.e. turn right if you were coming out of the shop). At the bottom turn left, soon passing the Manor House. On your right now is East Rand, mentioned in the note about Polgooth Mine; the stamps engine house is clearly visible, with its stack a little way up the tree-covered slope. At the corner with Trelowth Road was the main shaft of Polgooth Mine in the 18th century, and this is where the house built for the earliest beam engines would have been. A few yards past that on the left is a deep cutting, usually with pools in the bottom. This is in fact what in Cornwall was known as a "coffin" or "goffan" and in coal-mining country would be called open-cast mining; Hamilton Jenkin refers to it as "the great open-cut". It is presumably very old, probably pre-dating most of the shaft mining at Polgooth, and it provides a vivid illustration of one of the factors that made the mine so profitable, namely that many of the mineral lodes are at comparatively shallow depths. The coffin was once much longer than it is now: the far end of it has been filled in during recent years. (Not much further along the valley road is St Margaret's Holiday Park, where the engine-house of Polyear Mine is; it is not visible from the road, except perhaps in winter, so to inspect it you would need to seek permission from the owners.) When you reach Trecarne Close turn sharp left up a path running beside Rosemellyn Holiday Bungalows (St Margaret's Lane) and bear left where that joins the slightly wider Stony Lane. This brings you back to Trelowth Road. Turn left to look at the Old Count House, not much altered since it was the administrative centre of Polgooth Mine. According to Cyril Bunn's *Book of St Austell,* "As many as 2,000 miners were paid from the balcony above the front door in the mining heyday of the village." Joy Wilson's *Around St Austell Bay* has a photo of the house when it was the home of a coachmaker and wheelwright. Follow the sign to the post office, going up the narrow road known locally as "The Nip", which starts beside the Polgooth Press premises. The building housing the post office is, we were told, one of the oldest in the village; it was originally a farmhouse and later became a school - hence the little tower. A photograph of Polgooth exists - though I haven't seen it - which was probably taken from Mulvra Hill (on the east side) in about 1910, soon after most mining ceased, and apparently it shows hardly any buildings except the Manor House, the Count House and what is now the post office. It would seem that many of those 2,000 mine employees (women and children included) must have walked considerable distances to work, or that their cob-walled cottages in the village must rapidly have returned to the mud from which they came.

POLGOOTH MINE

It is often referred to as Great Polgooth Mine, and at certain periods it was called Polgooth United, Old Polgooth or Polgooth and Tregontrees. (So says Dines, though I wonder if it was really "Tregongeeves", the name of a nearby quarry and farm, and the home of Loveday Hambly, "the Quaker Saint of Cornwall" (1604-82).) "Old Polgooth" is certainly apt, because there is documentary evidence that shaft mining was being carried out here during the 1590s. Celia Fiennes visited the area in 1695 and wrote, "There were at least 20 mines all in sight, which employ a great many people at work almost night and day, including the Lord's Day, which they are forced to prevent their mines being overflowed with water. More than 1,000 men are taken up about them ....." *(Through England on a Side-Saddle)* Although she didn't name the mines, they were almost certainly at Polgooth. Before long most of the small mines had merged. In about 1720, Thomas Tonkin called Polgooth "the richest work this day in England or, I believe, that ever was in this Kingdom." At about the same time another writer referred to it as "this vast mine." In 1726-7 Polgooth acquired one of the first steam engines to be erected at a Cornish mine, a Newcomen engine with a 50-inch-diameter cylinder. A 63-inch Boulton & Watt engine replaced it in 1783. These engines were near the former count house, but as the mine developed more and more of the work was concentrated under Mulvra Hill, which divides the Polgooth and Pentewan Valleys; this area is especially rich in tin (plus some copper) because lodes running east/west intersect there with others running south-east/north-west. By the end of the 18th century there were said to be "no less than fifty shafts". For about fifteen years from 1807 the mine was closed (largely, it seems, because of disputes about smelting), but by 1823 it was under the management of John Taylor, who was at that time also breathing new life into the great Consols copper mine in Gwennap, and about to embark on the building of the Redruth and Chasewater Railway. The large engine house still dominating the area from the top of Mulvra Hill was built for an 80-inch engine capable of raising 1,000 gallons of water per minute: the second engine of such size to occupy the position. A smaller engine for winding was also erected on the hill, and a 25-inch stamps engine in the valley, linked to the working shafts by a tramroad with an inclined plane to the stamps. By 1837 Polgooth was reckoned to be the county's third largest producer of tin; but five years later it closed again because of low tin prices and from then on its fortunes were very chequered. In 1882 a larger stamps engine house was built, now being converted as a dwelling. All mining below adit level at Polgooth had ceased by the start of this century, but from 1902 to 1929 a reasonable living continued to be made by Thomas Sweet, who extracted valuable metal from the old dumps and shallow workings and processed it in and around the stamps engine house. Having spent some years mining in South Africa, along with his four brothers, he named his enterprise "East Rand". His grandchildren, Brendan and Pauline, still live there, and have done much to preserve and restore the water-driven stamps and other equipment Thomas used. A photograph showing him and his workforce posing beside the stamps is on page 25 of Peter Bray's *Around & About St Austell, 1880-1930.*

another engine house ahead - that of South Polgooth Mine (*).

4 At the road turn right, and after about 100 m. take the signed public footpath on the left, through a wooden gate. Quite soon (no more than 50 m.), cross the stile on your right, and go diagonally across the field, through the gap in the corner, and then walk beside the hedge on your right. Where that turns right, go straight on to a gate with a footpath sign. This brings you to a crossroads called Five Turnings.

5 Follow the sign to Polgooth. Just past the engine house, take the path on the left, which runs quite close to it. The mine buildings are surrounded by scrub, but there are one or two more-or-less overgrown, narrow paths which may enable you to take a closer look at them. If you do, please take great care, because they are in a fairly advanced state of decay. The ruined building with a corrugated roof on the left beside the track belonged to the mine and is said to have served as a carpenter's shop and miners' dry (changing-room). After the mine closed it was used as an abbatoir for a time.

6 To walk back to Polgooth, you could return to the road, but more attractive is to take the narrow path on the right just before you reach the wider track. On the right of it at the start is an old mineshaft. Soon you will reach a wider path with hedges both sides, Higher Coombe Lane. Turn left on that. It runs down into Polgooth, an attractive path if rather stony underfoot in places. Here and there you may notice boundary stones, because the lane marks the division between St Ewe and St Mewan parishes.

7 At the wide track turn right, passing a bungalow where ceramics are made and sold (Tara). The lane's name, Tyshute, may mean "house *(chy)* of the water-chute". Compare the Shute at St Day, which was till well into this century the town's main water supply: there are photographs of the water-cart being filled at it. The stream which may have fed the chute appears from the OS map to emerge from a mine adit (drainage shaft), but this is something I have not been able to check.

8 At the road turn left to return to the post office.

After I had finished writing the Polgooth walk I happened to come upon a very battered and butchered copy of *A Topographical and Historical Description of Cornwall,* published in 1810, by John Britton and Edward Wedlake Brayley. Here is part of their description of Polgooth, which I think makes a dramatic contrast with the quiet village of today, set among green hills.

> About two miles south-west of St. Austel is POLGOOTH, particularly distinguished by its extensive and rich tin works. The surrounding country appears for many miles bleak, desolate, and barren; but its bowels contain vast treasures, though, as a modern writer has observed, " like the shabby mien of a miser, its aspect does not correspond with its hoards." The shafts by which the miners descend, and through which the ore is raised to the surface, are scattered over a considerable extent of sterile ground, whose dreary appearance, and the sallow countenances of the miners, concur to excite ideas of gloom, apprehension, and melancholy.
>
> The number of shafts are not less than fifty, from twenty to thirty of which are constantly in use. The descent* into the

(Continued on page 10)

SOUTH POLGOOTH MINE

This was another ancient mine (its main lode, called Baldu or Baldue, is mentioned in a 16th-century document), but it never achieved anything approaching the size and prosperity of Polgooth Mine. Its deepest workings are only about 276 feet (46 fathoms, in the usual mining terminology). The engine house was built in 1880 for a rotary engine which was used both for pumping and to work 16 heads of stamps. The last active period of the mine was 1915-18, when arsenic was produced; the ruins can still be seen of the Brunton calciner, where ore was roasted, and the concrete-topped flue leading from that to the engine-house stack. For brief explanations of the processes involved in collecting and refining arsenic, and some comments about the uses to which it was put, see *The Landfall Book of the Poldice Valley* and *A Second View from Carn Marth.* A fascinating photograph of South Polgooth when it was producing arsenic is on page 50 of *Around St Austell Bay* (Bossiney Books). What an amazing transformation in less than seventy years!

WALK 3
THE GOVER VALLEY
Under two miles if based on Trewoon.
About four miles if walked to and from the centre of St Austell.

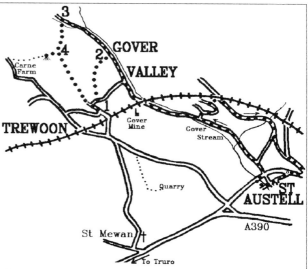

This is a beautiful and varied little walk in an area where old china-clay workings and quarries have been largely reclaimed by nature. If you start and end at Trewoon, the walk need take only an hour or so, although I think you will want to "stand and stare", especially on the second half, where the long views contrast with the wooded valley scenery that came before. Despite a fairly steep climb out of the valley, the walk is an easy one, if somewhat muddy at times. Trewoon has a pub and shops. Extending the walk to St Austell makes a pleasant addition. Recommended background reading for this walk is "Clay Country Remembered" by R.S.Best (Truran, 1986), one of the best-written (no pun intended) books of personal reminiscences I have come across.

Directions for a walk starting and ending at St Austell are given at the end. To base the walk on Trewoon (*), which is on the A3058 a mile or two west of St Austell or can be reached from the A390 via St Mewan church, take the right turning soon after you enter the village, Trevanion Hill, which is beside the Trewoon Garage and Stores. Roadside parking should not be hard to find on this small estate, but please be careful not to block entrances. Western National bus services 21 and 22 link St Austell and Trewoon: see current timetables.

1 Walk to the end of Trevanion Hill, which crosses the main London-Penzance line, and turn right on a minor road. After a short distance, take the footpath on the left, signed "Path to Gover". This delightful path, sloping gently downhill, runs between quite high leafy hedges, but provides good views over the Gover Valley (*), in which the stack and roofless shell of an old china-clay dry (Forest Dry) make a prominent feature, overlooked by a shapely little green mountain. (This waste heap and the adjacent pit are known locally as "Teddy Bear", but I must admit I don't quite see the resemblance. Charles Thurlow suggests that the name may come from the

16

TREWOON

The name is basically the same as that of Troon, south of Camborne, meaning "the farm on the downs". Although the old spelling has remained in use here, "Trewoon" is pronounced almost as "Troon", but with a hint of a second syllable: "Trooan". The Manor of Trewoon appears in the Domesday Book as "Tregoin". The parish church, St Mewan, is about half a mile south of the village; the oldest parts are Norman, but the bulk of the building is 15th century, heavily restored by the Victorians. Obtainable in the church is J.B.Lamb's excellent booklet, *St Mewan - Saint, Church and Parish,* which contains interesting information about Trewoon and Polgooth as well as the church itself.

---

nearby Trembear pit and hamlet.) To the right is the railway viaduct, with "Brunel's stumps" (*) alongside, and beyond that a glimpse of St Austell. Soon the path joins the entrance drive to a house named Trevanion Mill Cottage; nothing seems to be left of the mill itself apart from some ruined walls half-hidden by vegetation almost opposite the point where the path joins the drive. The house on the right at the foot of the drive looked brand new when we were there, but is in fact a converted chapel.

2 Turn left along the sandy track running up the valley, which soon passes a ruined cottage and the Gover Valley Kennels. The Gover Stream was quite fast-flowing, creating a series of small rapids, when we did this walk. At first, however, it can be heard but not always seen, as a result of the infestation of Japanese knotweed; and on the left are several rhododendrons of the rampant purple variety, *ponticum* - one of them determined to break into flower in late October! These, despite their beauty, are almost as serious a menace, since they create heavy shade, destroying smaller native plants that provide a much better wildlife habitat. Ignore the right fork in the track. The disused dry of Carne Stents works is on the left, but little can be seen from the track, apart from some high retaining walls. Later, at the point where there is a five-bar wooden gate on the right, keep to the main track, which now leaves the Gover and follows a tributary that joins it from the west. On the right, near the gate, is a ruined building including two grates, the remains of another old dry.

3 When you reach a small group of cottages, cross the iron footbridge on the left. A flight of steps now takes you quite steeply up, and soon you have a good view over the valley. Continue uphill on this narrow path among gorse and brambles. Coming into view now behind are the huge spoil-heaps of the china-clay works in the Hensbarrow area; on the right, crowned by several circular settling or de-watering tanks, is St Mewan Beacon. After the kissing gate, walk beside the hedge on your right.

4 At the second kissing gate, where you turn left down a tunnel-like track past Trevanion Farm to return to Trewoon, you could first walk a little way along the track on the right which leads to Carne Farm and St Mewan Beacon. Since the hilltop itself is not accessible to the general public, it's probably not worth going as far as the road just below it, but I would recommend a short diversion to the first gate on the left for the sake of the view. Perhaps you'd like to test your own local knowledge by trying to

THE GOVER VALLEY

"Gover" simply means "stream", so the name on the map, "Gover Stream", is a parallel to such examples as "Pill Creek" and "Penare Point". For decades it has been known locally as "The White River"; it is, of course, a tributary of the St Austell River, which was also given that nickname while it acted as a drain for china-clay waste. Even now the Gover Stream is often a bit cloudy: a little way up the valley it flows through a small pond that looks like milk with a turquoise tint. During the 1860s there was talk of extending the Pentewan railway through the Gover Valley to thriving works like Halviggan, Forest and Greensplat: John Lovering, who then owned the clayworks called Carne Stents in the valley, wrote in 1864 that "it would be a great thing for the port of Pentewan, that it would take nearly all the clay in the valley, viz. from ten to twelve thousand tons." Unfortunately, sufficient capital was not available. The Gover Valley is known locally as "The Stents", presumably referring to Carne Stents. "Stent" in china-clay terminology normally means hard-rock waste, but in this case it may have referred to tin (Cornish, *stean),* because tin was a by-product at Carne Stents. A small mine in the Gover Valley also produced some tin: see the directions for the extended walk to and from St Austell. R.S.Best's book *Clay Country Remembered* (see the introductory note) mentions that some Carne Stents workers were the first to come out on the occasion of the china-clay strike of 1913. The china-clay enterprises in the valley seem to have closed down a good many years ago; the Gover Clay Co., for example, closed as part of a "concentration" scheme to conserve resources during World War II.

Clay dry and viaduct, Gover Valley

name the most obvious landmarks, starting on the far right and working gradually leftwards: 1. the engine house with separate stack; 2. the village on the skyline; 3. another engine house on the skyline, this time with stack attached; 4. the deep valley leading down to the sea; 5. a third engine house, without visible stack, on a hill; 6. a church quite close at hand, its tower just visible among trees; 7. a small, ivy-covered stack on a hill, with a large waste heap on the right side of it. (You'll have done well if you know that last one, but all the others are visited or at least mentioned on walks in this book. The answers are at the foot of the page.)

'BRUNEL'S STUMPS'

Isambard Kingdom Brunel's broad-gauge main line from Truro to Plymouth, known initially as the Cornwall Railway, required the building of 34 viaducts, so he devised a relatively cheap design often called the "fan viaduct", consisting of stone piers with a timber superstructure. "Spider bridges" was another nickname often used. Viaducts of that type totalling nearly four miles in length were built during the 1850s, and even more were added soon afterwards on branches such as Truro - Falmouth. "It is generally supposed," wrote Canon Hammond in his *A Cornish Parish* (1897), "that these wooden bridges are precarious, and there have been people who would not take the railway journey through Cornwall because of their supposed insecurity. I believe that they are really safer than iron structures." And a footnote adds, "This is true of the beams, but some of the stone piers are said to be shaky. One in the Gover Valley (so one of the engineers assures me) moves when a train passes over it." Although in principle the design was perfectly satisfactory, the timber proved very costly to maintain, so when the need became apparent for the main line to be doubled the task of replacing Brunel's viaducts with all-stone or brick ones (or embankments, in a few cases) was undertaken, starting in 1871 and not completed till 1934. The Gover Viaduct was replaced in 1898; so too was the one in the Trenance Valley, which is known as the St Austell Viaduct, presumably to avoid confusion with Treffry's Trenance Viaduct at Newquay. The new viaducts were built beside the old, so that there needed to be hardly any break in train services. Most of the "stumps" of the old viaducts are still in place; some stone from the stumps at Gover was, however, used in the building of Forest Dry. Charles Thurlow tells me that workmen were stranded for a while on the top of a stump when a falling stone smashed their ladder. A detailed and fascinating account of the building, maintenance and dismantling of the wooden superstructures is given in *The Centenary of the Cornwall Railway* by R.J.Woodfin (1960).

ANSWERS

1. Ventonwyn Mine; 2. Sticker; 3. South Polgooth Mine; 4. the Pentewan Valley; 5. Taylor's engine house, Polgooth Mine; 6. St Mewan church; 7. Tregongeeves quarry, where there is a deep-looking flooded pit. A path leads up to the quarry from Meadow Park, the first right turning as you drive from Trewoon towards St Austell on the A3058.

TO START AND END THE WALK AT ST AUSTELL

From Fore Street walk down West Hill, a minor road starting at the roundabout opposite Globe Yard, which takes its name from a former coaching inn. Until 1833, when Truro Road was created, West Hill and Ledrah Road constituted the turnpike west from the centre of town. On the left are the Baptist Chapel and a former school, now part of the local College of Further Education. The northern terminus of the Pentewan Railway - see Walk 6 - was also on the left, lower down, near the three-arched 16th-century granite West Bridge, and one or two original buildings have survived; nothing remains, however, of the St Austell Foundry, which stood beside the railway yard, at the corner of Moorland Road: it was demolished about 1900. Its cast-iron nameplate is now at the Wheal Martyn Museum. Leo's now occupies the site of the old gas works, and Payless has replaced the workshops of the Cornwall Aviation Company. Cross the old bridge and turn right to walk beside the St Austell River. At the main road turn right, crossing the newer and much less attractive bridge carrying that, and turn left up Gover Road. Urban scenery soon gives way to suburban - and then rural, at the point where the road narrows and the pavement temporarily stops. Now there is woodland on the left, and the Gover Stream becomes more obvious. Beyond the bridge the stream is on the right, and there are no more pavements, but the road is usually quiet at this end.

Very well hidden among trees, shrubs and undergrowth on the left just before you reach the viaduct is the engine house of **Gover Mine**. Its recorded output, covering the years 1858-1881, was mainly iron plus some tin. According to Dines and Collins the workings were opencast, and this would suggest that the engine was to work the stamps. Kenneth Brown, however, has been told that "the engine used to work flat-rods through the viaduct into an adit on the opposite hill."

After passing under the viaduct, continue ahead, ignoring the left turning to Trewoon. At the entrance to White River Cottage, on the right, you have a good view of the stack of one of the many small disused clay dries in this area. The path from Trewoon joins this valley road or track from the left at the drive to Trevanion Mill Cottage; pick up the directions at point 2.

To walk back to St Austell later: the "tunnel-like track" mentioned at the start of point 4 ends on the edge of the housing estate; there turn left along a minor road which brings you back to the Gover Valley. Turn right, and soon you are walking under the viaduct again.

Rather than simply retracing your steps along Gover Road, after about half a mile you could go left up Turnavean Road. Keep on that as it curves right and left, and immediately before the entrance to No. 42 go up the path on the right, between a wooden fence and metal railings. This brings you to Trenance Road, which you join beside a pair of railway bridges: the nearer one, with rather beautiful brickwork, is presumably the newer of the two. An old china-clay works (Trenance Dry) is perched up above the bridges, and just beyond them is a loading bay with a small chute. Turn right, down Trenance Road, for St Austell. Now you have good views of the Gover Valley and Viaduct, and finally the road sweeps down past more of "Brunel's Stumps" beside another grand railway viaduct, this time crossing the St Austell River, hurrying on its way to Pentewan. Trenance Road joins Bodmin Road, which soon returns you to Fore Street.

WALK 4
A WALK BASED ON THE WHEAL MARTYN CHINA CLAY MUSEUM

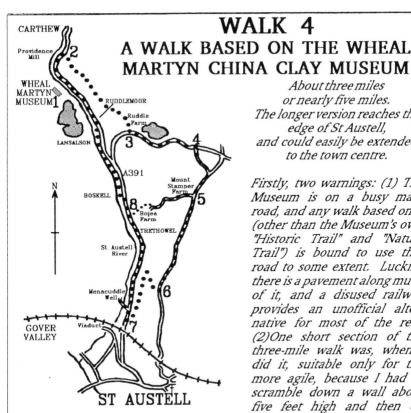

About three miles or nearly five miles. The longer version reaches the edge of St Austell, and could easily be extended to the town centre.

Firstly, two warnings: (1) The Museum is on a busy main road, and any walk based on it (other than the Museum's own "Historic Trail" and "Nature Trail") is bound to use that road to some extent. Luckily, there is a pavement along much of it, and a disused railway provides an unofficial alternative for most of the rest. (2) One short section of the three-mile walk was, when I did it, suitable only for the more agile, because I had to scramble down a wall about five feet high and then do battle with nettles and other vegetation before regaining the clear path. I have mentioned this problem to the Restormel Borough footpaths officer, and hope that improvements can be made. If you did attempt this route and get stuck (or come unstuck?) at that point, it's not very far to return to the road above, from which you could either complete the five-mile walk or retrace your steps to Wheal Martyn. These difficulties are, I feel, outweighed by the attractions of the walk, which gives a much clearer and more interesting idea of the setting of Wheal Martyn than could ever be gained from a car. The main road runs beside the St Austell River in a delightful wooded valley containing many relics of times past: small disused china-clay works; the railway mentioned above; at least two old corn mills, one of which has a recently-restored waterwheel; and a holy well in a magical setting, despite being within feet of speeding traffic. The rest of the walk is on higher ground which gives fine views, firstly of the other china-clay workings, old and new, which surround Wheal Martyn, and later of the coast and the lower end of the valley. The parts of the route that use tracks and paths are liable to be muddy. The going in general is quite easy: most of the steeper slopes are downhill. There is no pub or shop along the way, but the Sawles Arms at Carthew serves food, and is close to the route. Refreshments are available at the Museum between Easter and 31 October. The Museum café and shop can be visited free of admission charge.

WHEAL MARTYN MUSEUM

The Martyn family had bought land at Carthew in 1790, and built Carthew House a few years later. During a long and busy life Elias Martyn bought and developed many clay pits, among the earliest being Higher Ninestones and Wheal Martyn itself, and following his death in 1872 his son Richard Uriah Martyn continued the family business until his own death in 1887. In 1880, however, Wheal Martyn went into liquidation, to be taken over by Messrs John Lovering and Co.; under their ownership clay continued to be extracted from the pit till the depression of 1931, and the works remained in use till 1969, processing clay from other nearby pits. In 1971 the pit was re-opened, and clay from it is piped to other works for refining. A.C.Todd and Peter Laws in *The Industrial Archaeology of Cornwall* (1972) described Wheal Martyn as "perhaps the last small family clay works left in Cornwall where all the various hydraulic processes, Cornish lift pump, mica drags, settlement tanks and kiln tanks, dry and linhay, all within a small area, can be readily comprehended. .... This works must not be destroyed for it is a fine example of early clay technology." Only three years after those words were published the Museum was established on the initiative of English China Clays, with the support of many other bodies both local and national. The Museum incorporates buildings from the Gomm Clay Works, a smaller concern than Wheal Martyn, which operated from about 1878 till the 1920s. The *Historic Trail Guide* on sale at the Museum is an excellent companion, not only for a tour of the Wheal Martyn site, but also for a fuller understanding of much to be seen on walks in this book. See too Charles Thurlow's *China Clay* (Tor Mark Press), an admirably concise and well-illustrated study of traditional mining methods in Cornwall. Mr Thurlow tells me he is currently working on a similar volume dealing with modern methods. He also frequently leads a fascinating full-day tour of the china-clay region under the title of "The Pyramids of Cornwall", one of several "Mining Adventures" offered by Cornwall of Mine Ltd. For details, enquire at Wheal Martyn.

Directions are given from the Wheal Martyn Museum (*), which is between Ruddlemoor and Carthew, north of St Austell on the A391. Between November and Easter, when the Museum is closed, parking is likely to be possible in the two laybys on the left as you approach Wheal Martyn from St Austell. Western National bus services 29 and 30 run from St Austell and Bodmin to Wheal Martyn: see the current timetable. You could start and end the walk at St Austell town centre: see the end of the directions.

1 From the Museum's main entrance turn left along the main road. After a few yards there is a pavement on the right. Soon you will come to Providence Mill; the work on restoring its waterwheel was completed early in 1991. Providence was "so named after its chapel," says Canon Hammond. A photograph of this mill as it was in the early 1970s is included in D.E.Benney's *Cornish Watermills*, where it is called Carthew Mill.

2 Almost opposite the mill, take the footpath signposted sharp right.

Despite the high hedges, this farm track soon starts to give you interesting views: on the skyline to the right, the huge waste heaps at Greensplat and Hensbarrow; and in the valley the startling colours of the flooded pit of Lansalson China Clay Works beside the Museum - apparently turquoise milk surrounded by thickly-vegetated chalk cliffs and small green mountains! In the middle distance are the remains of two engine houses. The one that now lacks a chimney is on the Museum's Nature Trail; the other, at the Greensplat Works of Steetley Minerals, housed a 30-inch pumping engine which may have been built about 1830 (though 1850 is perhaps more likely) and which continued working until 1959, later than any other beam engine in Cornwall. It can now be seen at Poldark Mine, formerly Wendron Forge, near Helston. Interesting details about it and the task of removing and re-erecting it in 1972-3 are given in B.A.Fyfield-Shayler's book, *The Making of Wendron* (1979). Before long, the view ahead extends down the wooded valley, dotted with little, ivy-clad stacks, and there is a glimpse of the sea. Eventually you go through a gate and pass through the small farmyard at Ruddle Farm before reaching a road. ("Ruddle", by the way, is red ochre, a red earthy oxide which sometimes occurs in china-clay pits. Some iron oxide was sold as an iron ore.)

3 At the road, turn left. Cross and walk facing oncoming traffic, unless you are walking in a large group. Please take care: this road can be quite busy, and the curves on this part of it restrict drivers' vision. The trees and shrubs - many of them wild rhododendrons - restrict the views available to walkers, too; for example, a few hundred yards up the hill there is quite a large flooded pit on the left, used as a water reserve by the clay industry, but only the fencing gives you a clue to its presence, except perhaps in winter.

4 At the top of the hill, where a sign names Scredda, turn right on to a minor road. Now you have a fine view of the coast, with Gribbin Head prominent. At the T-junction turn right again. On the left here you have a good view of the Great Treverbyn sand tip. This was one of the last pyramidal tips formed by an inclined railway carrying sand from the bottom of the pit to the top of the tip. These heaps, also known as "sky tips", were once a distinctive feature of the clay landscape, but have now been superseded by the safer method, called "finger tipping".

5 The farm you soon come to is called Mount Stamper, a rather puzzling name because a hilltop is an unlikely site for water-powered stamps machines, and there is no record of steam-powered stamps here.

Now for the shorter route turn right on a made-up road with a gate across it - but bear in mind the warning I gave at the start. After the electricity substation the road becomes a track which curves left to Bojea Farm. The name means "lord's house" and is pronounced like a French word, "Beaujé". Don't go right down to Bojea farm buildings, but pass through the gap on the right when they first come into view (there was a fallen gate there when I walked this), and walk down by the hedge on your left. Now, unless improvements have been made to the path, there seems to be no alternative to scrambling down the wall ahead. From there, the way down to the bottom of the valley is clear enough, though probably rather overgrown: a rather rough track between hedges, then a kissing gate on the left, after which you cross a small field to a second kissing gate. At this point you cross the track of the disused railway by means of a few half-rotten wooden steps on either side. Finally a very narrow path beside a high fence brings you to a works entrance and the main road. Turn right on that, walking with extreme care, and pick up the directions at point 8.

For the longer walk, continue ahead at Mount Stamper Farm, along this minor road which keeps to high ground but unfortunately has few views because of the high banks. (On the other hand, if it's blowing a gale you may be quite happy to sacrifice the views!) After about half a mile it starts the descent to St Austell.

6 Where it curves left, just before you come to farm buildings turn right through a kissing gate on the right of a farm gate labelled Hill House Farm. After a second kissing gate on the left side of another farm gate the path descends steeply. Here you have one of the best viewpoints on the walk: up the valley almost to Wheal Martyn; ahead to luxuriant trees which in late October were stunningly beautiful (trees were first planted here by Charles Rashleigh, the creator of Mount Charles and Charlestown: Britton and Brayley in their *Description of Cornwall,* written about 1802, give a very detailed account of the "very considerable degree of persevering exertion" required to establish them on what had been "a coarse hill"); and left to the railway viaduct, St Austell, and, further off, the stacks and engine houses of Ventonwyn and Polgooth mines and the Tregongeeves quarry. A few steps lead down to a drive, on which turn left for the main road.

MENACUDDLE WELL

In his book on St Austell, A.L.Rowse calls Menacuddle Well "the very source and origin of the place, beside which perhaps St Austell ministered way back in the age of the Saints." Be that as it may, there is certainly known to have been a chapel beside this well in the middle ages, and the little stone building over the well, rated "one of the most beautiful in Cornwall" by A.Lane-Davies, is reckoned to be over five hundred years old. "One sees," comments Dr Rowse in another of his books, "where the tasteless restorers in our time have plastered a slate slab on the granite." Canon Hammond's history of St Austell includes a photograph of the building before restoration (page 298). The well-water has traditionally been credited with various powers: to give renewed strength to ailing children, to cleanse ulcers, to foretell the future, and to bring good luck to anyone who threw in a bent pin - or rather, in Hammond's view, to bring bad luck to one's enemies. He stresses the pagan origins of all this. Not the least attractive things about the well are its wonderful setting ("romantic" in Victorian terms)- a haven of peace and beauty within inches of roaring traffic - and its name. Attempts to explain it include Charles Henderson's suggestion, "Sanctuary of Guidel": Guidel is a saint honoured in Brittany, and Henderson thought it likely that the chapel was originally dedicated to him. In typical no-nonsense style, Dr Rowse merely gives "Rock-well", with no comment on either Henderson's theory or that of Oliver Padel, who sees the name as deriving from the Cornish, *meneth gwythel,* meaning "thicket hill" or possibly "Irishman's hill". (Bear in mind that Menacuddle is also the name of the farm on the hill to the east.) Cyril Bunn's interpretation is "place of the Irish monks", from *Menagh Codhal.*

7 Turn right on that; luckily there is a pavement. Before long, cross with great care to the little road on the left which leads down to Menacuddle Well (*), and from there goes up to the grand, turreted mansion called The Brake, now an old people's home. Canon Hammond claims that two sailors were once heard to observe that "a chap with that place and *three or fower pounds* a week could make hisself very comfortable." When you are ready to continue, return to the pavement, which continues as far as Trethowel, not far short of the point where the shorter route joins this road. A small, derelict and almost forgotten clayworks at Trethowel recently became the focus of much attention when an intact Cornish boiler was rescued from thick undergrowth there and transported with the aid of a traction engine, first to Roche in July 1990, then a few weeks later to St Agnes, next to Geevor, and finally on 21st September to Levant, where it will be used in the restoration of the whim engine, being carried out by the Trevithick Society under the auspices of the National Trust. The 1991 *Journal of the Trevithick Society* contains a description of the various interesting remains recently discovered at Trethowel, and also a detailed account of the history of the Trethowel China Clay Works, which incidentally also throws much light on the general industrial history of the Trenance and Gover Valleys.

Menacuddle Well

8 Soon you pass the remains of the bridge which carried the Trenance Valley branch (*) of the Great Western Railway. On the left just past the bridge is a converted watermill. On reaching the top of the hill, you can spare yourself further road walking by going through the wooden gate on the left to the track of the disused railway. (I must stress that this is not officially a right of way; it has been used by local people, but its owners, ECCI, have the right to close it to the public at any time.) Where you join it there seems to have been a station platform; this is Boskell, the point at which the line terminated after 1964. Soon the track becomes rather muddy as it runs beside the river, the latter masked by the ubiquitous Japanese knotweed. After passing two small, dilapidated clay dries (the Lansalson dries) and an ivy-covered stack, the trackbed reaches its original terminus, now a gravelled layby; and a little more road walking, partially on a pavement, returns you to the Museum.

THE TRENANCE VALLEY BRANCH LINE

By 1920 there were fifteen china-clay dries in this valley, operated by various works: Lower, Higher and South Ninestones, Trethowel, Ruddle, Wheal Martyn and Lower Lansalson. In that year the GWR opened a branch line from St Austell to serve the needs of these companies, with its terminus at Lansalson, close to Wheal Martyn. The dries at Bojea were linked to the line by a private railway, but the clay from the others had to be brought by cart in the early days, when over 100,000 tons per annum was handled; even so, by comparison with other routes it was never particularly busy. It was reduced in length in 1964 and shut down completely four years later.

TO BEGIN AND END THE WALK AT ST AUSTELL

Starting from the church, walk along Fore Street and turn right, up Bodmin Road. Soon after passing under the viaduct you join the route already described at point 7.

When returning, instead of turning right at point 6 (although it would still be worth going through the two kissing gates for the fine view over the Trenance Valley), simply continue down the road (Menacuddle Hill), passing, just before you reach the church, what A.L.Rowse regards as "by far the finest building in the town, after the church itself", namely the Market House. The lower floor of this was originally the Town Hall. St Austell Church is one of the loveliest in Cornwall, and no visitor to the town should fail to inspect it. The round walk based on St Austell would be about six miles in length.

WALK 5

TREGREHAN MILLS, CARN GREY
AND BOSCOPPA

Just over three miles.
For the sketch-map see the start of Walk 10.

I'm very tempted to claim that this is the best walk in the book; but then it was the last one I did, and the last one always seems the best. Even so, it definitely is something special: beautiful almost every inch of the way (the main exception being a few hundred yards through a housing estate: a good many inches there, I must admit), and full of historical interest. I suppose the glorious views are what most people would remember above all, but equally appealing to me was the pleasure of discovering half-hidden and unexpected relics of old mines and clay works. (Please note, however, that such sites are usually privately owned, and that to explore them may be physically dangerous.) It's quite an easy walk, although there are a few fairly stiff climbs - notably, of course, to the top of Carn Grey - and a good many muddy patches in a typical Cornish November, which is when I walked it. About a mile of the route is along a moderately busy main road, but to my surprise this made very pleasant walking, being downhill all the way and blessed with wonderful views ahead. There is no shop along the way, but the post office / store at Tregrehan Mills is close, and so are the shops at Boscoppa. The nearest pub I know of is the Britannia Inn, almost opposite the entrance to Tregrehan on the A390. By the way, if you have a copy of Rowse's A Cornish Childhood *and it's not too heavy or too precious to take out on a walk, bring it along and read the relevant part of Chapter VIII as you stand at the top of Carn Grey!*

The walk begins and ends at Tregrehan Mills (*), which is signposted from the A390, on the left a short way before the roundabout at the junction with the A3082 if you are coming from St Austell. Continue ahead over the crossroads and past the post office. Roadside parking is rather limited but should normally be possible opposite the playing field. Western National bus service 24A (St Austell - Par) passes through Tregrehan village: see current timetables.

1 Continue north along the road, with the stream (locally known as the river) on your right at first - rather hidden by the dreaded Japanese knotweed, but very plainly audible, at least in November. Soon the road crosses the stream, and the marshy ground on the right here marks the site of one of the two former mill ponds. A "shoot" or spring of good drinking water still issues from a pipe in the hedge near the gate to "Brookside". Beyond that comes woodland, and soon an old stack peers out from the foliage. It served a china-clay dry a short way to the south, to which it was connected by a long flue; the remains of that run beside the road for several yards. A few feet from the stack is Maudlin's Well; its name is presumably a corruption of Magdalene's, but I have seen no reference to it in books about

TREGREHAN MILLS

The mills have gone now, but Valerie Brokenshire's excellent little history of the village, *A Village Portrait* (1985), explains that there were two. Mill ponds on both sides of the road north to Trethurgy, close to where the stream passes under it, fed a leat which ran on the far side of the present football field, and that powered a corn mill first, then flowed on to work a bone mill in the woods near Boscundle, on the far side of the Bethel-Bodelva road. This mill has now been converted into a residence called Carpenters Barn. Mrs Brokenshire says, "the mills of Tregrehan have existed for a very long time, certainly from 1486-1906." The water in the leat was also used at various times to work the stamps of small mines. Referring to Tregonissey in *A Cornish Childhood*, A.L.Rowse writes, "It had never produced anybody known to history, or with an approach to a name. Tregrehan Mills even had produced a Samuel Drew." That "even" shows how insignificant a place it was reckoned to be. Samuel Drew, born in 1765, was a "buddle boy" at a local mine at nine and apprenticed as a shoemaker about two years later. He became famous as a preacher in the Methodist Church, and also as a writer of books and articles on metaphysics: a scholar, "endowed," as his memorial says, "with a powerful intellect". A well-known history of Cornwall by Fortescue Hitchens was edited by Drew in 1824. He died in 1833. Methodism flourishes at Tregrehan still, and Mrs Brokenshire tells me she believes the local chapel holds a record for one of the last surviving Sunday School anniversary feast days - an old tradition. It is held on the Thursday following the first Sunday in July, and features a procession, brass band, saffron buns, a public tea and sports.

holy wells. Valerie Brokenshire (see the note on Tregrehan Mills) writes that people used to travel long distances to use this water because of its reputation for purity, and that this well was the source of the first piped water laid on in the village. She also mentions, however, that it drained from old mine workings, so my first impression - that this was an old adit - may not be completely wrong. The workings in question were those of Tregrehan Mine or Wheal Joney, which became part of Wheal Eliza Consols (*). A short way up the hill behind still stands the ruined engine house, built in about 1890 for a large rotative beam engine; once it was a prominent landmark, but now trees shroud it, and it is not accessible by public footpath. Only a few yards further along the road is another old stack up on the right, this time clearly part of a disused china-clay dry (Vounder). Just a short way further up the road, on the left, is what the OS map calls an "aqueduct", with a sluice gate; this leat or launder passes over the stream heading westwards. In November it was gushing with rather milky water. If you're willing and able to scramble up the bank on the right you will see where the water comes from: a small waterfall now, but there was once an overhead launder feeding a waterwheel in the wheelpit. According to information supplied to Kenneth Brown by Mr John Tonkin, the wheel was working at least till the late 1920s, and drove pumps at Carvear claypit, several hundred yards to the east, by means of flat-rods running through the adit-like tunnel close by. (Carvear is now part of Bodelva pit.)

WHEAL ELIZA CONSOLS

This group of mines, some of them quite old, included Boscundle, West Par Consols, Blue Gate, New Wheal Eliza and Tregrehan Consols. (Just in case that list hasn't confused you enough, I'll add the fact that some of those mines belonged to another group called Charlestown United before Eliza Consols was formed. The many and sometimes very slight variations of names adopted by mining companies create some of the most dangerous traps for the unwary historian of Cornish mining.) From 1864, Wheal Eliza and West Par Consols had been owned by the same company, and made huge profits by exploiting a rich tin lode that lay beneath the grounds of Tregrehan Manor: see the note on Tregrehan, Walk 10. In 1884 they employed 190 workers underground and 111 at surface. Tregrehan Mine, once known as Wheal Joney, is quite a long way north of the other mines that formed Wheal Eliza Consols, and seems to have been added to the group at a late stage: the only recorded production before this century was ten-and-a-half tons of black tin in 1889-93. According to D.B.Barton, Wheal Eliza Consols closed in 1892, having survived to a later date than any other mine in the St Austell area. In 1908 a new attempt was made to work Wheal Eliza and Tregrehan, but this lasted only till 1913. Dines says there was "practically no production" during that period, but Collins mentions 3 tons of black tin from Tregrehan in 1909, sold for £196. Kenneth Brown tells me that a lot of evidence of the work done at this period remains at Tregrehan Mine, in the area around the engine house and the main shaft higher up the hill to the east. A ruined engine house survives at the Wheal Eliza sett, and a short walk to visit it is suggested at the end of the directions.

---

2 Where the road bends left (approaching another old clay dry, Garkar or Garker), go up the signed Public Bridleway which soon crosses the stream. On the right at first is the leat, and you can see where it emerges from a tunnel. This leat is of special interest, because it was built in the late 1790s by Charles Rashleigh to carry water from Cam Bridges in the Luxulyan Valley a distance of at least six miles to Charlestown; there it fed two reservoirs, and the water in them was used to keep ships in the dock afloat at low tide, and also periodically to flush sand and other waste out to sea. The system is still, I believe, in working order. For more details see the note on Charlestown (Walk 9), and also Walk 12 in *Around the River Fowey.* Continue up the track and then turn left through a five-bar wooden gate, opposite a metal gate and just before the entrance to The Barn, Vounder ("lane") Farm. After a muddy patch, the path goes steeply uphill and then runs above a pretty valley. Although the view is restricted compared with what is to come, it already includes much of the coast from the Gribbin to Black Head, with a glimpse of Bodelva clay works behind and Carn Grey ahead. A small wooden gate brings you to an ECCI parking-place; ahead, beyond a black gate, is the attractive flooded pit known as "Hennals", now a fishing pool. Turn left on the sandy road, with a small stream on the left along part of its length.

3 At the road, turn left past the Trethurgy Wesleyan Chapel. (Rowse's explanation of "Trethurgy" as "the village of the water-dog," i.e. otter, is thought by Padel to be much less likely than "farm of Devergi", a personal name.) A short way back to Tregrehan Mills would be to continue down this minor road; but for Carn Grey take the first right turning, where there is a sign to Chytan Farm, and bear left at the main road.

4 Opposite Carne Grey Cottage, take the path on the right. From here there is a rather confusing choice of paths and tracks, but you just need to keep going uphill, past an impressive flooded quarry pit, to the rock-pile beside another flooded quarry pit at the top of Carn Grey (*). The view to the south requires no comment; to the north and west it is cut off by the big Carclaze (*)clay works, with its monitors (high-pressure hoses) at work, and its long conveyor belt taking waste to a distant tip. The path continues on the south side of the pit to return to the road, where you turn right. Please walk with care: the traffic can be fast here.

5 Take the first left turning, signed to Bethel (named, I presume, like the Bethel at Twelveheads, from the founding of a chapel). The road, which soon takes you past the Civic Amenity Site, is called Menear Road, referring to the prehistoric menhir or longstone, six feet tall, which can be seen from gateways on the left just past the Amenity Site. This road is rather less busy than the other, but care is still needed. Walk facing the oncoming traffic (unless you are in a large group): it is safer, and in this case also provides you with much better views than the motorists are able to enjoy. Eventually you descend to the edge of the modern development of St Austell known as Boscoppa, though the original place of that name is further east. The road names on the right - Hallane, Trenarren - call to mind another walk.

6 Turn left at Killivarder Way, whose name presumably recalls a long-lost wood *(kelli,* grove). Keep to this road till you come to a T-junction at the bottom.

7 Turn left there, past Bishop Bronescombe primary school, over or beside a cattle-grid, and along a rather rough but attractive tree-lined lane. After a few hundred yards, notice the old stack a little distance away on the right, attached to the ruins of an engine house. Boscoppa, described by Dines as "a small mine in killas country" (that is, where the mineral-bearing lode ran through sedimentary rock rather than granite), is recorded as having produced 27 tons of black tin during the 1870s, and a little more from openwork in 1899. It was probably worked by just two men. Soon you reach Boscoppa Farm, with its attractive old outbuildings in a beautiful setting, looking towards the coast across what was once Boscoppa Downs and Boscundle Common. (Valerie Brokenshire writes that "Boscoppa Downs had many mines, and leading from Mr Allen's farm at Boscoppa is a labyrinth of tunnels, adits and shafts. It is said that when the mines were all working one could walk from Boscoppa to Crinnis underground.") The track goes to the left of the old ruined manor house of Boscoppa and becomes a narrower path running through woodland. Soon you cross a small footbridge and are back more-or-less where you started. The old house set back on the right as you join the road, Kaslo Cottage, was, says Mrs Brokenshire, the count house for Wheal Joney where the ore was assayed.

CARN GREY

As I hinted in my introductory note to this walk, Carn (or Carne) Grey features in A.L.Rowse's autobiography, and I would not presume to try to emulate his description of the view from it or of the special magic of the place. "In whatever mood of temper or impatience I left home," he says, "I came back from Carn Grey at peace with myself, happy." Highland areas like this were almost certainly occupied in prehistoric times, and it is hardly surprising that legends about pagan rites have attached themselves to this place: one of them avers that Bronze Age people used the flat rock on the top of the rocky outcrop for sun worship, and sculpted the stones below to make an anticlockwise stairway up to it; another assures us that between about 700 and 200 BC Phoenician traders conducted Baal-worship here - hence, according to Cyril Bunn in his *The Book of St Austell,* the nickname of "the Baal Stone" for the flat rock, and of "Baal" for the Carclaze pit. He also mentions the legend that "when St Mewan was preaching on the Carne Grey Rock, rain began to fall, and he and St Austell took shelter under the overhang of the rock." However little truth there may be in such tales, it is certain that there were at least two barrows just south of the hill, and a site only a little way north at Trethurgy was occupied by a circular earthwork which seems to have been inhabited from about 250 to 550 AD; excavations there in 1972-3 revealed the remains of five round houses and other buildings. Why the carn is called Grey I don't know; perhaps from a personal name, or because of the colour of the rocks (compare the various headlands with names like "Caragloose", not all of which look particularly grey to me). Stone was quarried here until 1939.

Gribbin Head from Carn Grey

CARCLAZE

The name helps to confirm the importance of this area to prehistoric man: *cruc glas,* "green barrow". J.H.Collins (1912) says that according to local people the site was mined for tin as early as the reign of Henry VII. By about 1830 it was the largest and most famous openwork mine in the county. In that year the pit was said to be six acres in extent, with eight stamping mills at work, and shafts sunk 60 feet below the bottom of the pit. T.Allom's well-known "romantic" engraving of Carclaze (1831) is included by A.L.Rowse in his *St Austell,* and in coloured form by Embrey and Symes in *Minerals of Cornwall and Devon.* One of the best descriptions is that by George Henwood in *Cornwall's Mines and Miners;* this dates from the late 1850s, by which time Carclaze was already concentrating entirely on the production of china clay. Henwood's description of the view from Carclaze is also worth reading, and makes an interesting comparison with the one by Rowse mentioned in the note on Carn Grey.

A POSSIBLE LITTLE "EXTRA": WHEAL ELIZA

Although a path runs beside the ruined engine house of this once-important mine, it does not fit conveniently into a round walk. If you would care to visit the site, you could park near Boscundle Lodge, which is on the right as you drive south from Tregrehan Mills to the A390. Watch for the public footpath sign. You may be able to park on the little bungalow estate close by. The path runs straight ahead, uphill, and the pumping-engine house stands among trees on the left after three or four hundred yards, where another track forks left. The separate stack and a capped shaft are a few yards along that track. Return the same way.

FOOTNOTE : "WHEAL JONEY"

The following was set down by Dr J. Penderill-Church and has reached me via John Tonkin and Kenneth Brown. I would not care to vouch for the literal truth of every colourful detail, but in essence it may reflect what many small and struggling Cornish mines were like. It is also of a piece with another tale told locally about Wheal Joney, "that the miners brought tin from elsewhere and propped it in position to convince the captain to keep working it." (From Valerie Brokenshire's "A Village Portrait")

During the 1870-73 tin boom there was some small scale activity, after which the mine remained idle until 1881, when a little ore was extracted by a mine captain and three assistants. This was probably "Captain Joney". After 1883, the mine was not worked again until 1889, when Captain Joney resumed operations with an old man or two and a couple of boys. To start with, he actually did cut sufficient ore to yield 10 tons of black tin after stamping at the King Stamps, but with the proceeds from the sale of this he adjourned to the local hostelry, the Britannia Inn. Soon he got fed up with digging out tin, and thought of a little method of whiling away the time more profitably, although he did cut a little ore from time to time, to show there was no ill-feeling. He advertised shares in the mine, and arranged a very clever system to fool the shareholders. He kept one old man at the mine to tend the engine, while two boys kept watch at the Nettles Corner junction. The shareholders at this period always arrived by Carriage, and as soon as the boys saw them coming, one boy would run like fury up to the mine to wake up the old man, to get the fires lit in the engine-house, while the other would run for all he was worth to the Britannia Inn, and rout out Captain Joney, who took a short cut across the fields to the mine, adjusting his collar and brushing his top hat as he went. When the shareholders arrived at the mine, after having wet their whistles at the Britannia, they would find Captain Joney waiting to meet them, and the engine-house chimney smoking cheerfully. After they had departed, Captain Joney returned to his normal habitat again. His activities earned the mine another local nick-name - that of "Britannia Consols", it being said that the inn ought to be one of the mine's major shareholders. This state of affairs lasted until 1893, when presumably the shareholders must have got wise to him.

At Polgooth, near the start of Walk 2

The Trenance Valley at Menacuddle, Walk 4

Carn Grey, looking north (Walk 5)

Looking south-west towards Polrudden on Walk 6
Penare Point in the distance, Point of Well closer

Valerian at Pentewan, Walks 6 and 7

Part of the old harbour on Pentewan sands

A steep section of the coast path, approaching Black Head on Walk 6

Duporth beach, Walk 9

WALK 6
MEDIUM AND LONG WALKS BASED ON PENTEWAN
Just over three miles or nearly six miles

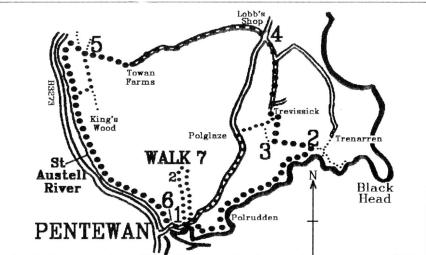

As the large number of boxed notes related to the longer version of this walk implies - and they do little more, to be honest, than scratch the surface - it is one of exceptional historical interest. In terms of scenery, too, it is beautiful and varied, including some fine cliffs, two lovely but very contrasting valleys, woods and high, open farmland. As usual, the coastal section is the most strenuous ("the only cliffs in Cornwall which have absolutely defeated me," declares J.R.A.Hockin in Walking in Cornwall - but they're not nearly as bad as they look!); if after walking the coast you'd rather not undertake the full route, the medium-length alternative offers a comparatively easy return to Pentewan, using a road which carries a moderate amount of traffic in summer but compensates for that by being mostly downhill and commanding good views. Roads, apart from extremely minor ones that rarely see more than the occasional tractor, are almost completely avoided on the longer walk. A recommended "extra" would be to explore the woods in the Pentewan Valley, which have quite recently been opened to the public. Pentewan has toilets, shops and a pub, and these are the only such facilities en route; if you plan to start the full-length walk in the morning and have lunch at Pentewan, you could use one of the car parks provided for visitors to the woods, on the left of the B3273 as you drive south from St Austell (grid references: SX 007497 [just past the concrete products works south of London Apprentice] or 006487), picking up the directions part-way through point 5. The valley path described in section 2 is likely to be muddy, and in wet spells very muddy indeed; an alternative route through Trenarren is suggested. See also the comments in section 3 about a muddy stream that has to be crossed on the medium-length route.

PENTEWAN

Pentewan and the Pentewan Valley are fascinating places to explore, particularly for anyone interested in tin streaming, the china clay industry, ships, harbours and early mineral railways. In the directions and other boxed notes I have given a few hints about what there is to see, but the history of the area is so rich and complex that I cannot hope to do it justice in the space available. Luckily, several leaflets and small books are easily obtainable locally which will enable you to understand how Pentewan developed and how all the observable details fit into a pattern. For a very brief outline, get *A Short History of Pentewan,* written by K.M.Batchelor for the local Old Cornwall Society. *About Pentewan and Pentewan Valley,* produced by the Pentewan Valley Chamber of Commerce, includes many fascinating snippets about the area generally as well as the particular businesses featured. *Pentewan* by R.E.Evans and G.W.Prettyman is an interesting and well illustrated 32-page booklet clearly set out in sections. Best of all for an understanding of the docks and railway is M.J.T.Lewis's *The Pentewan Railway;* but if you don't have the time or inclination to delve as deeply as Mr Lewis does, do at least take a close look at his plan of Pentewan in 1906 (page 13): this, together with the section on Pentewan Block and Sand Works in *Pentewan,* would go a long way towards enabling you to interpret the details. For a more personal angle, try *Rail and Sail to Pentewan* by John Henry Drew, the recollections of a footplateman on the mineral railway whose father was the engine driver from 1887 till 1913. See also Liz Luck's brief but evocative portrait of the village in *South Cornish Harbours.* One thing I will add which you won't find in any of those is that the sand-bar on Pentewan beach frequently makes an appearance on television, because it was chosen by Lloyds Bank in October 1989 as the setting for its commercials featuring the black stallion galloping along the shore. In fact, two stallions were filmed, Concara and Beatos (the latter had to have his white "socks" painted out), and two pretty mares were strategically placed in order to spur the males on!

Directions are given from the small free car park almost opposite the Ship Inn at Pentewan (*). See the start of Walk 7 regarding buses.

1 Start by walking past the pub, toilets, village square (two other pubs used to be in the square: The Hawkins Arms now transformed to Piskey Cove, and The Jolly Sailor probably now the Post Office Stores), and the harbour basin, and up Pentewan Hill. Turn right at The Terrace (*), at the far end of which a sign indicates the coast path. All along the part of it included on this walk you will have a sturdy fence topped with barbed wire to your left, but fortunately this first bit is the only one where you are hemmed in closely on both sides and made to feel like an enemy threatening invasion. Just in case you happen to be slow on the uptake, a notice warns you not to trespass on the cliffs and fields of Polrudden (*). What looks like a tiny coastguard lookout hut stands on a high point not far from the farm buildings; beyond that, the path curves around Polrudden Cove and climbs to the top of the high cliff on the far side, where the quarries are - not only to the left of the path, but in the cliff-face too. Richard Carew mentions that Pentewan stone was

THE TERRACE

The little Anglican church of All Saints and the delightful houses with their long colonnaded verandah owe their existence, like so much else in Pentewan, to Sir Christopher Hawkins, and date from 1821, but some things here are much older. For example, many of the windows of the houses look Tudor or Jacobean, and it seems probable that they and some of the stone in the walls were taken from the ruins of the old house at Polrudden. Part of the south wall of the church may be even older - possibly Norman - , and the remains of arches at the back of the houses lend weight to the belief that this is the site of a small monastery. An old name for The Terrace was Monks' Walk. The new church was apparently little-used as a place of worship, and became a carpenter's workshop for a time, but was re-opened as a church in 1878.

POLRUDDEN

Perhaps indeed the fear of invasion does haunt those who live at this farm.

> John Polruddon
> All of a sudden
> Went out of his house one night,
>
> When a privateer
> Came sailing near
> Under his window-light....
>
> They saw his wine
> His silver shine
> They heard his fiddlers play.
>
> "Tonight," they said,
> "Out of his bed
> Polruddon we'll take away."

Charles Causley's poem goes on to tell how they "bore him down the height"; he never returned, and the great house fell into ruins. The story was first written down by John Norden early in the 17th century. A.L.Rowse in "The Story of Polruddon" *(West-Country Stories)* speculates that John Polruddon (pronounced "Polreddon", says Rowse) acquired his wealth from the highly-valued Pentewan stone quarried on his land, from the Duchy of Cornwall Freestone Quarry. It was used in St Austell, Fowey, Lostwithiel, St Sampson's (Golant), Bodmin, Mevagissey and other churches, as well as mansions such as Trewithen. Polrudden has a special place in the history of Cornish mining as the site of the first attempt in the county to smelt copper on a commercial scale (1690-7). In view of the remoteness of Polrudden from the main copper-producing areas it's no surprise that the enterprise failed. Copper smelting requires very high temperatures and therefore uses much more coal than tin smelting, so the great centre of the British copper-smelting industry was South Wales.

"digged out of the sea cliffs" *(The Survey of Cornwall,* completed by 1602). At low water the remains can be seen of a jetty where the stone was loaded direct on to barges. It looks as if it must have been a risky operation, and indeed in 1830 when J.T.Austen (later called Treffry) was obtaining stone for his new harbour at Par, three of his vessels were wrecked while loading at "Clift Quarry", Polrudden. Soon after the quarry comes a steep descent and an almost equally steep rise: 53 steps to climb. In the distance ahead is Black Head, and just this side of that is Hallane beach. First there is a path down to another small beach, and the coast path drops to a wooden bridge over a dry stream-bed (dry in August, at least); then comes the big climb to the top of the most impressive cliff in these parts, called The Vans (Cornish, *ban,* peak). It's a long haul but not horribly steep, and perhaps you will have strength enough to peer down at the natural arch in the cliffs as you climb, and to notice that Carlyon Bay beach and the church spire at Charlestown are visible across the promontory when you finally reach the top. Daniel Lysons *(MAGNA BRITANNIA, 1814)* refers to "an oval camp, called *The Van",* and indeed this does seem a very likely site for a prehistoric settlement. Now a flight of steps helps you down the steep slope. Soon you are walking through beautiful woodland, and reach a bridge over a stream.

2 Here turn left to continue the walk (unless you want to visit Hallane beach and Trenarren first: strongly recommended. See Walk 8.). Now you are on a narrower path that runs beside the stream up a lovely wooded valley. Here and there the path may be a little overgrown. *(If the valley path is too muddy, you could avoid it by walking up through Trenarren and continuing on the road to Lobb's Shop; there turn left for the direct way back to Pentewan, or for the full walk follow the directions from point 4.)* There are three gates to go through while you are among the trees, and then you enter an open field. Keep to the bottom of the slope, passing a tiny pump-house delivering water to the farm above, till you reach a metal gate.

3 Mr Roger Treleaven, who farms Trevissick, informs me that before long a new path will be opened up from this point. It will involve going through the gate and then following the small valley curving slightly to the right. The new path will meet the existing track where it fords the stream (see • below), and there signs will direct you left for Pentewan (3-mile walk) and right for Porthpean (longer walk, via Trevissick farmhouse). In August 1991 the only practicable route from this point was *not* to go through the metal gate but to climb the steep hill on the right, keeping beside the hedge to your left at first, then continuing over the brow of the hill. When Trevissick farm buildings come into view, make for the farm gate to the left of them. Go through that and turn left.

FOR THE THREE-MILE WALK: go past the open-sided barn and then turn sharp left into a field. Follow the obvious track as it curves downhill, fords a muddy stream (•) where you are likely to be glad of a pair of wellies unless you are prepared to get wet feet, and continues uphill to a kissing gate beside the road to Pentewan; turn left on that. The road, like most others in these parts, is protected most of the way by high banks or hedges, but there are fine views ahead as it begins to slope down towards the village, and near the entrance to Polrudden farm look right for a glimpse of Glentowan in its little valley, visited on Walk 12.

FOR THE LONGER WALK: follow the cob wall as it turns right. This takes you past Trevissick (*) farmhouse. Go straight on along a minor road, and on joining a slightly wider one still continue ahead.

TREVISSICK

The farmhouse is believed by Mr Treleaven to date back to the 13th century, although the front was rebuilt in Queen Anne's time following a fire. A.L.Rowse, who includes a photograph of the house in *St Austell,* refers to the "big Jacobean hall-kitchen at the back". Trevissick farm's land now stretches from just north of the old quarry at Polrudden to Silvermine Point, not far south of Porthpean (more than three miles of the coast path), its western boundary being the road running south from Lobb's Shop towards Pentewan. Once, Mr Treleaven told us, this territory was divided among five farms and supported 22 people; now it is just one farm run by four people, and in present conditions even those four are hard-pressed to make a decent living out of it.

---

4 Next comes the "main" road to Pentewan, Porthpean and St Austell. Cross that and walk past the few houses that make up Lobb's Shop - presumably once the site of a blacksmith's shop. Not surprisingly, the hamlet seems to have played a part in the activities of smugglers using the nearby small beaches: "We know," writes Mary Waugh, "from the reminiscences of a gardener then (i.e. during the 1830s) employed on the Penrice estate that all sorts of illegal happenings took place at Castle Gotha and Lobb's Shop..... The insatiable demands of the local miners ensured a ready market for the spirits landed at all these beaches." *(Smuggling in Devon and Cornwall,* 1991). This little road - hardly more than a farm lane - runs along a ridge, so the occasional gaps in the roadside banks offer wide views. It is called Towan Road, and it ends at the twin Towan (*) farms, East and West. (See the boxed note for information about the holy well at Towan.) Go through the gate ahead, cross West Towan's farmyard, and keep more-or-less straight on along the main track, ignoring the one that branches off to the left. Soon you have a fine view to the right, including St Austell and, further left, the engine house of Great Polgooth mine, perched on its hilltop. On reaching a metal gate ahead, take the grassy track on the right - very attractive but liable to be muddy, especially where it begins to slope down more steeply into

---

TOWAN

If you read the historical notes made by Thomas Tonkin (died, 1742), you may be surprised to find Towan described as "the chief place" in St Austell parish. Towan was the head farm of the Saxon royal manor of Tewington, which appears in the Domesday Book as Dewintone, and was one of the seventeen Cornish manors included in the Duchy of Cornwall when Edward III created the Duchy in 1337. It was therefore an administrative centre with its own manorial court or "leet", and this led William Hals to declare that "Tewington" (or Towington or Tawington) means "*silence in town* or *extraordinary silence in town,* viz. when the court sitteth" - which is fairly typical of early efforts to interpret Cornish names. Tonkin rejected this theory, mentioning the common meaning of *towan* (sand-dune), but preferring "hillock" for this particular place. Oliver Padel in *Cornish Place-Names* adds a further suggestion, that the St Austell River might once have been called the Tewyn, which is similar to the name of a river in Wales, and could mean "bright, shining river". That would make better sense of the name Pentewan as "foot of the Tewyn" rather than "foot of the sandhills". Lake's *Parochial History* mentions a baptismal well at Towan, "over which is an ancient building .... in the early English style of architecture, covered with an arched roof granite." The well is now dry, but its Pentewan stone building was restored by the St Austell Old Cornwall Society in 1937 and has been maintained since then by the farmer at East Towan, on whose land it stands. Known locally as "the wishing well", it is not visible from the public footpath, but you may be able to get directions to it at the farms. It is also known as "the chapel well"; there is no sign of a chapel here now, but some old field names seem to confirm that there was one, and the great student of Cornish saints, Canon Doble, has suggested that both chapel and well may have been dedicated to St Touinianus .... thus offering yet another possible explanation of the place names!

Peckhill Wood. It looks like an old route, sometimes running in a cutting with mossy banks, and we wondered if it had once been used by packhorses. The owner of East Towan farm told us that in his grandfather's time - 50 or more years back - horses were used to haul timber up it. Eventually it brings you down to a small parking space where there are gates into the woods: Shepherdshill to the right, Peckhill and King's to the left. (King's Wood had belonged to the Crown until the execution of Charles I; in about 1650 it was purchased by the Sawle family of Penrice.)

5 Here another choice presents itself: either (A) go down fairly directly to the riverside path, or (B) get to it by means of the rather more winding and probably muddier paths through the woods.

FOR (B): go through the gate or over the stile on the left side of the parking space. Walk along the wide track for about 300 m. and then take the narrow path down on the right (unless, of course, you want to explore the various tracks and paths in King's Wood first). Now all you need to do is keep heading downhill towards the sounds of traffic on the main St Austell - Pentewan road. Probably the easiest route is to take the slightly narrower path on the left where the main one starts to curve right. After a short scramble down you will reach a small stream (actually a leat, as explained later). Go left a few yards and cross this by means of the plank (if it's still there!), then turn left and soon you will reach the riverside path, just south of a second small parking space. Turn left for Pentewan, and continue reading after the next paragraph.

FOR (A): Continue down the main track (not through either gate). Ignore the first left turning, but just after crossing a small stream (really the same leat as mentioned above) take the next track on the left, which soon brings you down to the river, where you turn left. After about half a mile on the riverside path you will reach a second small car park near a bridge - one of the "official" entrances to the woods. Still continue on the riverside path.

You are now walking down the Pentewan Valley. The river is given as the St Austell River on the maps, but old names for it include Clissey, Gover and Winnick or Vinnick (the last two probably meaning "stony"), and until quite recently it was usually known as the White River because of the huge tonnages of china-clay waste that found their way into it as it flowed down from Hensbarrow, discolouring not only the river but also the sea, which only a few years back was commonly milky in appearance well out into St Austell Bay. The river is clear now (all discharges of china-clay residues since 1973 have gone to special mica dams or worked-out pits), although in parts it's often hard to tell, because of the jungle of Japanese knotweed which is rapidly colonising it. This section of the riverside path, running along a small embankment, marks the course of the Pentewan Railway (*), but about a mile north of Pentewan harbour the line curved east, leaving the riverside. Running down the valley a little east of the river is a leat (millstream), actually the tailrace carrying away the water that once turned the waterwheel at Molingey Mill near London Apprentice. Rather than return the water direct to the river, the long tailrace was cut to provide power at the Wheal Virgin Streamworks (*), and later it served to fill the reservoirs which were dug in order to flush out the harbour. (See the note about Pentewan Harbour.)

THE PENTEWAN RAILWAY

In several of my earlier books I have written about the first two railways to be built above ground in Cornwall: the Poldice Plateway or Tramway (1809) and the Redruth and Chasewater Railway (1825). Only three years after the latter was built, work started on a single-track line of about 4ft. 6in. gauge designed to enable freight to be carried efficiently between St Austell and the new docks at Pentewan, and by June 1829 horses were drawing wagons along it, although in fact the gentle gradient enabled much of the seaward trip to be accomplished by gravity, as *The West Briton* reported in 1830: "four wagons linked together with about fifteen tons of china clay on them, are put in motion at the depot at St Austell by two men gently impelling them .... Their speed gradually increasing, ... they proceed with the celerity of a mail coach, ... the man who has charge of them having to put his horse to a gallop in order to keep up with them. Having arrived at level ground, ... the conductor attaches his horse to the foremost carriage, and they are thus drawn to Pentewan wharf where a greater quantity of china-clay is shipped for Liverpool, Scotland, &c. than from any other port in England." Locomotives were not introduced until the 1870s, when the gauge of the track was reduced to 2 feet 6 inches. China clay was, from 1873 onwards, loaded into vessels from a low trestle viaduct on the south-west side of the harbour basin; the main freight carried inland was coal, which was loaded into the wagons from the opposite side, near the Ship Inn. The railway played a vital role in the local economy, but its fortunes fluctuated with those of the docks, and the masses of sand deposited by the St Austell River frequently disrupted the operation of the railway by causing the river to flood. The worst disadvantage it suffered from was that it did not reach the china-clay pits it was designed to serve, and road transport (namely, horses and carts) always had to be used to link them to the St Austell terminus. Closure came in 1918, when the Government requisitioned the engines, rolling stock and track as part of the war effort. Some of the buildings at St Austell West bridge terminus may still be seen.

6 The path enters Pentewan opposite a former smithy which later became a cattle-shed and coal store and is now "The Tree House". Turn left. Notice the small sluice-gate on your left, once part of the flushing-out system I have just mentioned. Soon you will come to the car park, the Ship Inn and Pentewan Harbour (*) - not, perhaps, one of the most attractive harbours in Cornwall, but it has rightly been called "a fascinating natural museum of industrial Cornwall" (Brenda Duxbury: *About Mevagissey*), and as such it is well worth exploring.

WHEAL VIRGIN STREAMWORKS

Although the Hensbarrow area, where the St Austell River rises, is best known now as a producer of china clay, it has also been an important source of tin, and for millions of years alluvial tin has been deposited in the Pentewan Valley. As explained in Walk 5, the Polgooth district had some of Cornwall's greatest tin mines, and for several centuries the tin deposits in the valley were enriched by waste washed down from there. William Borlase (1758) called the Pentewan Valley "the most considerable stream of tin in Cornwall." There were several small and ancient streamworks at the St Austell end of the valley, one of which, at Trewhiddle, became famous late in the 18th century when streamers discovered a hoard of Saxon silver. Two larger streamworks operated near Pentewan: one called Happy Union, on the west bank of the river not far above the beach, and the other called Wheal Virgin, about half a mile upriver from there, on the east side. Both were apparently flourishing by 1780, and may have been very much older than that; tin streaming was probably carried out on the Wheal Virgin site as much as 3,000 years ago, to judge by the discovery in 1852 of a shaft considered by archaeologists to date from the Bronze Age. It was lined with oak timbers and hurdles of oak twigs, and the top of the shaft was 3 metres below the 1852 surface. In the previous year the Wheal Virgin streamers had found a beautifully-made and well-preserved wooden tankard with a bronze handle, and this is thought to have been made in the 1st century AD. It can now be seen in the Royal Cornwall Museum in Truro. Just in case you imagine tin streaming to have been a variation on panning for gold, I ought to point out that the tankard is thought to have been found nearly 30 ft. below the surface; at Happy Union the "tin ground" was even further down, probably as much as 54 ft. (14 ft. of silt, 20 ft. of sea sand and a top layer of 20 ft. of river gravel); and to reach those depths all the streamers had was shovels and wheelbarrows. Add to that the labour involved in raising the tin-bearing gravel to surface, preparing the ore for smelting, and keeping the workings reasonably dry, and you will see why George Henwood (1860) described streaming as "an avocation .... requiring a hardihood of frame not often found in underground miners." In fact, of course, tin streaming did sometimes involve underground mining, as for instance in Restronguet Creek, and this evidently applied to Happy Union, which was visited in 1783 by Rudolph Eric Raspe, creator of Baron Munchausen. He wrote that he saw there "a very well organized underground tramroad", and this has been claimed as the first railway to be built in Cornwall. A plan of Wheal Virgin, dated 1861, shows two shafts and a level nearly 70 feet deep. Happy Union seems to have closed in 1837, but Wheal Virgin continued till about 1874; both made an important contribution to the silting which so plagued Pentewan harbour. The normal practice of the streamers was to back-fill as they dug out new tin-ground; that explains why there are no obvious deep holes left in the large areas they worked. For a detailed account of tin streaming methods and the discoveries made in the Pentewan Valley, see *Tin in Antiquity* by R.D.Penhallurick.

PENTEWAN HARBOUR

Fowey was a natural choice as the southern end of "The Saints' Way" when that footpath was devised (see *Around Padstow* and *Around the River Fowey)*, but Pentewan might well have been picked instead, because it too was on a prehistoric cross-county trading route. Its cove was therefore an important beaching-point from very early times, and that importance grew with the increasing popularity of Pentewan stone and the boom in the fishing industry. A small harbour was built in 1744. The mineral wealth of the Pentewan valley, where rich deposits of alluvial tin had been streamed for centuries, and of the high land from which the St Austell River flowed (tin and china clay), convinced Sir Christopher Hawkins of Trewithen (see Walk 2), who owned much land in and around Pentewan as well as china-clay works, that Pentewan needed to be converted into a modern, efficient port. Work started in 1818 and took eight years: the old harbour basin was enlarged and deepened, new quays were built, and dock gates and cranes were installed. Two other things that were done are particularly significant. Firstly, a small reservoir was built just north of the basin, fed by the stream flowing down the little Glentowan valley; the hope was that sand and silt collecting in the harbour basin and entrance channel could be flushed out periodically by opening the reservoir's sluice gates. Secondly, a 500-foot-long jetty was built on the south side of the harbour entrance, in order to steer the water of the St Austell River as far away as possible from the harbour. But neither the reservoir nor the jetty could overcome the problems created by the millions of tons of waste pouring down the river from the stream works and clay pits, and the history of Pentewan harbour is dominated by the ceaseless battle with the sand. In 1831 a 160-foot breakwater was added to the jetty; in the 1870s four new reservoirs were built, this time in the main valley, fed by the leat from Molingey Mill, as mentioned in the directions. These and other measures brought at least short-term benefits, and the harbour did have several busy and prosperous periods, but a report in *The West Briton* of 28 February 1862 describes an all-too-common situation: "In Pentewan Creek sixteen small ships have been detained for five weeks to the great loss of their owners and others concerned. These vessels draw from eight to nine-and-a-half feet of water, and they cannot get out in consequence of a sand bank having drifted into the channel...." No cargo vessel has entered the harbour since 1940, and even then only the entrance channel could be used. For a much fuller account of the history of the harbour, and information about the industry which grew up from about 1900, selling sand from the beach and using it to make concrete blocks, read *Pentewan,* by R.E.Evans and G.W. Prettyman. The rails which can still be seen near the old quays are relics of that enterprise; so too are most of the unlovely buildings on the south side of the harbour basin, now used as workshops and the local sailing club's headquarters.

Pentewan harbour

WALK 7
A VERY SHORT WALK AT PENTEWAN
About a mile

> We did this walk during the exceptionally soggy June of 1991, and we were only about a quarter of the way round when the heavens opened. We hastily donned our rainwear, and within five minutes the limitations of its ability to hold the floods at bay had been cruelly exposed.... It must say something about the attractiveness of this little walk that we both remember it with pleasure. Even without the delights of water dripping and splashing from every leaf, I'm confident you will find it an enjoyable way to spend an hour or less of your time at Pentewan. The route is shown on the map for Walk 6.

Pentewan is south of St Austell: take the B3273 road. There is a fairly frequent "Hoppa" bus service between St Austell and Pentewan. Directions for the walk are given from the car park almost opposite the pub.

1 From the car park, walk past the pub and turn left along Glentowan Road, passing the Village Hall. Go through the gate ahead and up the narrow path on the left, as directed by the Public Footpath sign. Soon you are walking up an attractive valley, with a good view of the sea behind. After about a quarter of a mile you will reach the deserted and semi-derelict buildings of Glentowan. For some discussion of the meaning of the name, see the note on Towan in Walk 6. Glentowan was built as a shooting-lodge for the Sawle family of Penrice, later became a farmhouse, and has now been unoccupied for over forty years.

2 Just past Glentowan you are presented with a choice of three paths. Take the middle one. Go through the gate into woodland. Now the path continues on the right, descending gently at first, then steeply. At the bottom, a few stepping-stones should help you cross a muddy area without too much squelching. Beyond the stile there are more - and better - stepping-stones, and then the path, as it reaches the east side of the valley (known locally as "The Brake") becomes shady, almost tunnel-like; so, at least, it seemed during that June rainstorm. The O.S. map indicates "Quarries (dis)" and an "Adit" in this area. Perhaps these are visible from the path at a time of year when the foliage is less luxuriant. An adit is a shaft designed to drain the water from mine workings; most adits come to the surface on cliff-faces or in valleys like this. What mining took place here I don't know, and it is possible that this adit drained the quarries. There are some comments on the quarries north of Pentewan in the note about Polrudden, Walk 6. Gradually you will emerge into the open as you head south, and after passing through a gate you are back in the village, passing the pretty terraced cottages of North Road, called The Row when they were built for the quarry workers. The largest building was one of Pentewan's three limekilns. On reaching the harbour turn right, past the public toilets, to return to your starting-point.

WALK 8
PORTHPEAN, CASTLE GOTHA, TRENARREN AND THE COAST

Almost five miles; or the route could be split into two round walks of about half that distance: see point 3 in the directions.

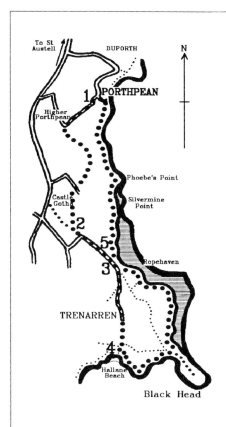

The stretch of coastline included on this walk is very beautiful, and even the inland parts of the route offer many fine views of the sea and the cliffs. The small villages of Higher Porthpean and Trenarren are both delightful, Trenarren being especially idyllic. Traces of two Iron Age fortified settlements are to be seen. This part of the coast has several steep ups and downs, so you might prefer to make two walks of it. The car park at the entrance to the Ropehaven nature reserve just above Trenarren (grid reference SX 033489) is ideally placed for the short walk around Hallane, Black Head and Gerrans Point, and would also be a suitable base for the other short walk (Silvermine Point, Porthpean and Castle Gotha) or the complete 5-mile walk, but for these I have suggested you use the car park above Porthpean beach, because that would mean you could get refreshments at the end of the walk during the season, from the beach café. There are several small, attractive and easily accessible beaches along the way.

Porthpean ("little cove") is signposted from the St Austell bypass road (A390), about half way between the roundabouts at Mount Charles and the Asda superstore. Soon after the entrance drive to Penrice Hospital, take the left turning signposted to Porthpean beach. There is a car park just above the beach; out of season this may be closed, in which case you will need to find a roadside parking spot. Alternatively, you could drive back up to the top road (either via Higher Porthpean or back along the road you have just come down) and follow the signs to Trenarren. Just above Trenarren is a small car park, from which you could pick up the walk directions at point 3. There is no bus service to Porthpean; Charlestown, nearly a mile away via the coast path, is served by "Hoppas" from St Austell.

1 On leaving the Porthpean car park, turn right, passing the sign Higher Porthpean. The steep, narrow road soon brings you up to the pretty little village, with its attractive chapel-of-ease (St Levan's Church), spoilt only by the rusty cowl on its chimney. It was built in 1884 at the instigation of Sir Charles and Lady Graves Sawle of Penrice. (The pre-eminence of the Sawles in local society is illustrated by a story told by Canon Hammond in his history of St Austell. "A lady in one of our Sunday Schools asked a boy in her class "who was the first King of Israel?" As he did not know, she presently informed him that it was King Saul. "What, Sir Charles?" said the youth, in open-eyed astonishment.") The village square still has its old pump, but the post office indicated on the O.S. map is now "Post House", and the school (another gift of the Graves Sawles) is now "Old School House"; not far away are farm buildings, many of them now looking rather dilapidated and empty.... Evidently Higher Porthpean was once a lot livelier than the sleepy village we wandered through on that hot August day, where not even a cat or dog stirred, let alone a human being. Walk past the pump, Post House and Old School House, and at the entrance to Court Cottage, where a notice announced "Honey for sale", take the narrow path down on your left. Go through the metal kissing gate (the first of many on this walk: I was tempted to christen it "The Kissing Gate Walk", but in the end I didn't have the neck.... Some puns are too bad even to deserve an apology.) Follow the obvious track that runs parallel with the cliff-edge, just a hundred yards or so above the coast path. Kissing gate 2 is in a hedge on your right, beside a Public Footpath sign; cut diagonally across the field this gate admits you to, heading just right of the farmhouse. Soon you will see another footpath sign on the skyline ahead: make for that. Cross the farm lane after negotiating kissing gate 3 and go through kissing gate 4. (This is where I feel the kissing has to stop! From now on every gate on this walk is of the kissing variety unless otherwise stated.) Cut across the left-hand corner of the field to gate 5, continue across the next small field to gate 6, and then still in the same direction down the much larger field to gate 7.

At this point, before passing through gate 7, you could turn quite sharply back, at an angle of about 45° to the line you have just been walking, in order to look at the remains of Castle Gotha (*). Look for another kissing (sorry!) gate in a hedge, with a dry ditch curving off to the right of it. This is part of the ancient "castle"; most of the rest has disappeared beneath the plough. The view, both coastal and inland, which you get from the other side of the gate, makes it clear why our ancestors chose this site for their settlement. Return the same way to gate 7 to continue the walk.

CASTLE GOTHA

Evidence from digs during the late 1950s and early 1960s suggests that this site was occupied for 300-400 years, from the second century BC to the second century AD. The people lived in stone or wooden huts, and many of them seem to have been metalworkers; there also appears to have been a workshop handling the local Pentewan stone. Most of the rampart and ditch have been ploughed out, but the oval-shaped enclosure was apparently rather more than a hundred yards across at its widest, with its entrance to the north-east. A very detailed account of the excavations at Castle Gotha was published in the 1982 issue of *Cornish Archaeology*.

---

2 Beyond that gate, walk beside the hedge on your left to gate 8, which brings you to a minor road. Here you have a delightful view to the left of a deep valley (later you'll be scaling the sides of that one, so reserve some energy!), and across to the beach at Carlyon Bay. Continue ahead along the road, which has high banks at first but soon gives you a superb view eastwards to Gribbin Head, not far from Fowey. Soon you will come down to the small car park just above Trenarren, beside the entrance to the Cornwall Trust for Nature Conservation's Ropehaven Cliffs Nature Reserve. This consists of 49 acres of cliffs and broadleaved woods in an oustandingly beautiful setting, and particularly in winter it is an excellent vantage point for observing bird life.

3 *Here you could follow the coast path sign at the near end of the parking space, thus omitting Trenarren and Black Head and reducing the walk to about two-and-a-half miles; but if you do that, I hope you'll be able to return another time and do the other half, which if anything is even more attractive. For the shorter route back to Porthpean, pick up the directions at point 5.*
For the complete walk, continue down the road past Trenarren House, the home for many years now of the Cornish historian A.L.Rowse, and through the charming hamlet of Trenarren (*), whose pretty cottages were thickly bedecked with flowers when we were there. ("Adorable" is Rowse's choice of adjective for Trenarren, in "The Story of Polruddon".) When you reach

A cottage at Trenarren

51

TRENARREN

The name appears to mean "Crane Castle" - or possibly "Heron Castle", since according to Oliver Padel "the two birds were not strictly distinguished in practice". The first syllable probably derives from *dyn,* a fort, rather than from *tre,* a farm or village, and presumably refers to Castle Gotha, although Black Head is closer. Once Trenarren was much larger, and had two pubs plus several shops. In his *St Austell - Church: Town: Parish* (1960), A.L.Rowse writes of the Hext family who in 1618 took up residence in the manor house in "this exquisite, sheltered valley", "a paradisal, though not particularly profitable, place to settle." They built their Georgian house, further uphill, in 1810. A photograph of it is included in the book. In *A.L.Rowse's Cornwall* (1988) he says it was built in 1805, and mentions how he "longed to live there".

---

the entrance to Hallane House, continue downhill on the track to the right, which soon becomes a pretty woodland path. It's worth going on down past the coast-path signs, beside Hallane Mill to the delightful little Hallane beach - a real sun-trap on that August day, and almost deserted. It is indeed, as Martin Collins says in his *South West Way,* "a superb picnic spot", but unfortunately it tends to be a trap for floating oil as well as sunshine, so I advise you to watch carefully where you sit. Care is required when bathing, too, because of the many submerged rocks.

4 Return to the coast path signs. If you are interested in watermills, you may care to go a few feet along the path to the left to see where the millstream crosses it; the waterwheel itself, of course, has gone. To continue the walk, however, follow the coast path sign to the right. Soon you are climbing quite steeply, and have a view to Pentewan beach; on reaching the stile at the top you see Black Head, and before long you will have to decide whether to walk out on to it. It would be a pity not to: the views from it are very fine. When you are near the tip you feel as if you are on a small island, and it's easy to understand why it was chosen as the site of a settlement in Iron Age times. There are traces of three lines of defence across the neck of the headland, the most obvious of them being two ramparts over 5 m. high and a ditch 2 m. deep, all on the left side of the path as you walk out. On the same side are the remains of a rifle range: two shooting platforms and a metal contraption, the target butts. It all looks as if it fell out of use many years ago, but according to the relevant National Trust leaflet (*Coast of Cornwall,* No. 20) it is still used on alternate Sundays in winter, when "due notice is given and red flags (are) flown." Something of the flavour of life in these parts over 150 years ago is captured by a short item from *The West Briton* of May 1835: "On Thursday the 14th instant, the crew of the preventive boat stationed at Porthpean, "crept" up (trawled up with grapnels) 125 tubs of contraband spirits, sunk by smugglers, off the Blackhead, and lodged them in the custom-house sheds at Fowey."

Back to the coast path now, which ascends a short flight of steps and continues along the top of very shaly, insubstantial-looking cliffs. Ahead now in the distance are Porthpean beach, with a large white house, Porthpean House, above it; Duporth "holiday village" above another beach; and, a little further right, Charlestown, with its docks and spired church. The path curves left near Gerrans Point - a rather surprising name in view of the fact that Gerrans village is a good many miles southwest, near Portscatho. Perhaps this place has some association with the 8th-century Cornish "king" or chieftain, Gerent, who supposedly lived at Dingerein Castle in Gerrans parish. Now the woods of the Ropehaven nature reserve come into view, with several attractive little beaches below them. The remains of fish cellars still exist at Ropehaven, and the foundations of harbour walls can be seen at low tide. The name appears on some old maps as "Ropehawn" or even "Ropehorn". After some steps downwards, the coast path turns left (the path ahead leads to the first of those beaches) and then rises quite steeply before curving inland to the small car park just above Trenarren. Cross the stile at the far end of the car park.

5 The coast path now runs above the woods of the nature reserve, and soon goes steeply down to a bridge over a stream in a deep gully. The stream falls to a silvery little beach below. "Silvery" came to mind because the small headland ahead is called Silvermine Point. Roger Treleaven of Trevissick, who farms most of the coastal area from Polrudden (near Pentewan) to this point, told us he had never come across any evidence of mining here; on the far side there is a cave just above high-tide level which could possibly conceal an adit (drainage channel), but I have not explored it. A.K.Hamilton Jenkin says "an adit is known to exist at Silvermine Point", and suggests it may be a relic of Wheal Neptune, an unsuccessful attempt to mine copper between 1812 and 1821. 78 steps bring you almost to the top, where there's another stile and a good view of Porthpean beach. "Porthpean," writes Canon Hammond, "was much addicted to smuggling - many is the lugger (it is said) that has been run ashore here. The contraband goods would be carried away inland by mules, over whose track a drove of sheep would be driven to obliterate their footprints." Next comes a lovely sweep of clifftop fields; keep to the edge. Another deep valley follows, with a natural arch at Phoebe's Point. Soon you are descending towards Porthpean. In 1991 part of the path here was blocked and diversion signs were in place; at the point where we rejoined the official path we had to duck under barbed wire or climb an awkward fence. I trust that this obstacle will have been removed by the time you do this walk.

Porthpean House has a steep three-acre garden noted especially for its collection of two hundred camellias, as well as for its show of primroses in early spring. It is occasionally open to the public in aid of charity: for details see the current issue of the Gardens in Cornwall Open Guide. *Porthpean House is owned by the Petherick family, of whom A.L.Rowse writes: "The St Austell tradition is that the founder of the family fortunes walked out of Cornwall on foot all the way to Cumberland, where he found an extremely rich tin mine and made a large fortune."* (St Austell: Church - Town - Parish)

Silvermine Point (Walk 8)

WALK 9
PAR, CARLYON BAY AND CHARLESTOWN

About six miles; nearly eight if extended to Porthpean.
Could be done as a walk of three to four miles, returning to Par by bus.
For the sketch map, see the start of Walk 10.

I hesitated about including this in the book, mainly because of the difficulty of making a satisfactory "round walk" of it: the area immediately inland is quite heavily built up or occupied by private woodland and a golf course, and threaded through with busy roads and the main railway line. I also supposed that the coast here was rather unexciting, and spoilt by modern industry and large-scale "leisure" complexes. On the other hand, to leave out Charlestown would have been unthinkable .... So we dutifully set off from Par on a clear, crisp October morning, and enjoyed the coastal walking far more than we had dared to hope: it is full of variety, provides superb views both along the coast and inland, and if it is less dramatic than other sections it atones by being less strenuous. Charlestown did not disappoint: its very special magic can best be appreciated from the coast path, if not from a boat. The problem of the return route remained, and I am not wholly satisfied with the one I am about to offer, because too much of the first part is on roads, and the rest is the same as the end of Walk 10. The views from that particular stretch are very fine, however, and there are compensating factors even on the earlier inland section. Even so, you may prefer to walk back along the coast or use public transport: the St Austell Hoppa Service No. 31 links Charlestown and Par. See the current timetables. Par and Charlestown have pubs and shops, and during the season refreshments can be obtained at the "Cornish Leisure World" and Porthpean beach. There are several pleasant bathing beaches along the way.

Directions are given from the Par Inn: see the start of Walk 10. East-to-west is the better direction to walk this section of the coast path unless you want to have the steaming chimneys of Par in your sights most of the time.

1 From the Par Inn walk south, that is, along the main road to St Austell, with a railway line and the Par River on your left. Soon you pass under the main London-Penzance line, carried by a rather unusual bridge with arches within its arches. Next come the huge ECCI "dries" with their gleaming silver stacks, and then the main entrance to Par Harbour: see the note in Walk 10. (The name "Par" itself means harbour or cove.) Take the fenced path on the left just after the traffic lights at the second railway bridge. Notice on the right, beyond the bridge and the road, disused china-clay dries (now used as stores) with ivy-covered stacks, and a line of circular concrete settling or de-watering tanks on the hill above them. Where the path crosses a footbridge you are close to more such tanks, some circular and others rectangular, and then you come to the edge of the golf course.

2 On reaching the coast, it's worth going left first for a ground-level view of the harbour. (You get a bird's-eye view later if you do the full round walk.) On the seaward side of Treffry's great breakwater is Spit Point, a Mecca for

CRINNIS

It is almost unbelievable now that the area around the Carlyon Bay Hotel was for a few years the site of one of the world's most productive copper mines: Crinnis, later called Great Crinnis, or Great Crinnis and Carlyon Consolidated. When it was started in earnest, in 1811, it was called Crinnis Cliff Mine: the adit (drainage channel) opened out at the foot of the cliffs, and some mining was carried out under the sea. The OS map indicates a disused shaft close to the cliff edge a little way west of the hotel; but the workings extended inland at least as far as Crinnis Wood, where rather more extensive remains are indicated. Some prospecting had been done in the area a little earlier, and Captain Joseph Michell, whom Jenkin describes as "an experienced and reputable miner", is now best remembered for stating in 1808 that the property was "not worth a pipe of baccy". By October 1812 the mine was producing about 600 tons of rich ore per month; in 1813 25-30 pack mules were employed carrying ore down to Charlestown harbour: "no such mine was ever known before in Cornwall," declared a newspaper correspondent at that time. One of its exceptional features was that the great body of ore lay quite close to the surface. This proved a mixed blessing: an article in the *Mining Journal* reported that "the various offices of the establishment sunk to the depth of many fathoms, giving the appearance of an earthquake." The mine's success was short-lived. Trouble was brewing by about 1818 when the various adventurers (shareholders) who had lost interest before 1811 began trying to lay claim to a share of the huge profits: see the interesting extract from *The West Briton* of 3 April 1818, included in *Life in Cornwall in the Early Nineteenth Century,* Bradford Barton 1970. Legal actions went on for years, involving also the neighbouring East Crinnis mine, over which the Duchy of Cornwall claimed mineral rights. (It is said that in that action, documents weighing three-quarters of a ton were brought in evidence, and that the 130 witnesses consumed "370 grogs and 50 bottles of wine" on one evening alone.) Well before these matters were settled, the best lodes at Great Crinnis had been worked out; the mine struggled on for a few more years before closing (Jenkin and Barton seem to disagree about the date of closure). Further attempts to work it were made in the 1850s and 1870s, but with little success. By the period when A.L.Rowse's mother was a child - presumably about 1870 - many of the old workings of Crinnis were already out of sight and out of mind. She told him "of the tennis party given at Crinnis House (where a younger generation of Carlyons was living at the time), in the course of which the tennis lawn collapsed, there being a shaft beneath. Then there was the neighbouring farm of Mrs Hicks's, where they had all been to help about the hayrick which was constructed for shelter right beside the house. Next morning, when they got up, it had disappeared - also down a shaft." *(A Cornish Childhood)*

lovers of rock pools. Return the same way for the walk to Charlestown, starting above Spit Beach along low cliffs of silvery slate which are quite rapidly being eroded. The view ahead now, if it's clear enough, stretches to Chapel Point, just past Mevagissey, with a glimpse of the Dodman above it; closer is Black Head; Porthpean and Duporth beaches can be seen, but not yet Charlestown harbour. The Carlyon Bay Hotel is prominent. Inland are St Austell and, closer, St Blazey Gate (Biscovey) with its spired church. Gradually the cliffs, with small quarries scooped out here and there (though some of the cavities may result from natural cliff-falls), become higher as you walk above the long Crinnis (*) Beach. Inland, notice the seat of the Carlyon family, Tregrehan, among woods: see the note in Walk 10. Now you are entering the realm of the "Cornish Leisure World", "The Entertainment Capital of the West". As you approach the vast warehouse-like building which is the beating heart of that great enterprise (though there have been a few cardiac arrests lately), keep to the edge of the golf course until a sign directs you further left. When you reach the road, unless you feel irresistibly drawn to your left continue over the zebra crossing, beside the car park, and across the mown greensward that decorates the view from the Carlyon Bay Hotel. (The official path presumably keeps to the right-hand edge.) Just before the path briefly joins Sea Road opposite the Porth Avallen Hotel there is a good view-point on the left, from which you can get your first glimpse of Charlestown harbour. The nearest headland is called Appletree Point; not a likely-looking spot for fruit-growing, but Cyril Bunn mentions a local saying that the white monks who once owned land in this area had an orchard here. Somewhat later than the monks' day it was mined, mainly for copper;

A china-clay vessel entering Charlestown dock

Dines's short note on Appletree or South Crinnis Mine refers to "extensive old workings", "said to reach 100 fms. below adit" - that is, 600 feet below the drainage shaft, the portal of which is presumably in the cliff just above high-tide level. Records of the mine's output cover the period 1849-66. Now follow the acorn signs, and soon you are descending towards Charlestown (*). The stack inland is part of the Charlestown Lower Dry, now disused. There are toilets just above the harbour. The Rashleigh Arms is a short way inland, not far beyond the Shipwreck & Heritage Centre.

3 It's well worth continuing along the coast path, even if only for the views of Charlestown which you get near the start. Part-way up the fairly steep climb there is an excellent vantage-point for watching china-clay vessels inching their way round the impossibly-tight-looking corners at the entrance to the dock. Beyond the first two kissing gates there is a good view of the old china-clay dry. After the third gate the path runs through woodland above Du Porth beach. The name means "two coves" or "two harbours", presumably referring to "big harbour" (West Polmear, Charlestown) and "little harbour" (Porthpean). A bridge takes the coast path above the lane linking the Duporth Holiday Resort to its beach. The Georgian Duporth House was built by Charles Rashleigh as his country home. Its grounds were described in 1882 as an "earthly paradise". "It is all now," acidly comments Dr Rowse, "quite appropriately to the age *we* live in, a holiday camp." *(In the woods above Carrickowel ("high rock") Point beside the blue notice about dogs on beaches there is a path to the road which would provide a possible return route to Charlestown, but it is a good deal longer than the coastal walk and is entirely on roads which tend to be busy. The road down into Charlestown is, however, attractive, especially the lower end of it. It enters the village almost opposite the pub.)* As the coast path runs down to Porthpean beach there is a garden area with seats on the left, and a short way below that is an unusual little concrete building, a World War II watch-house. The final descent is by quite a steep flight of steps. Unless you want to continue to Black Head (Walk 8), return to Charlestown by the same route or the alternative I have mentioned; and at Charlestown if you are walking rather than bussing back to Par, start by retracing your steps along the coast.

4 Where the path joins Sea Road, for the inland route continue on the road. This makes quite pleasant walking: it is evidently a "select" residential area, with well-kept gardens and what John Betjeman would probably call "villas". At the end of it, after passing the Carlyon Bay Hotel, you could return to the coast path by going down the road on the right which leads to the "Leisure World", or to stay inland continue ahead along the private road which has the golf links on the right and soon passes under the main railway line. The bridge, built in 1859, is in the "Gothick" style, perhaps in deference to the wishes of the Squire at the time - a Carlyon, presumably.

5 On joining the main Par - St Austell road (A3082), turn right. Luckily there is a pavement to use.

6 Take the first left turning, Pennys Lane, an attractive little country road. Just beyond a long, low bungalow (Lilac Cottage), turn right on to a grassy track. Continue ahead through the kissing gate. On the far side of the field you now enter are a disused mine shaft and ruins of buildings including the

CHARLESTOWN

In 1790 this was a fishing village (total population: 9 persons), known as Porthmear, Polmear, or West Polmear to avoid confusion with Polmear north of Polkerris. There was no harbour, but already some china clay was being shipped from the beach: in that year, for example, four vessels bringing in coal and limestone and taking china clay and china stone had suffered damage in the process. Twelve months later, a period of rapid change had begun, as a result of the enterprise of Charles Rashleigh. Born in 1747 at Menabilly (the mansion near Gribbin Head that was to become the home of Daphne du Maurier) and trained as a lawyer, he settled at Duporth (with a town house in St Austell, now the White Hart Hotel) as a successful businessman with interests in china-clay and mining. Armed with plans he had commissioned the famous engineer John Smeaton to draw, he first had a pier built, and then over the next few years thousands of tons of rock were excavated to make room for two basins, a dry dock, warehouses, a ship-building yard and dwellings. A hotel, a rope manufactory, cooperages, limekilns, a brickworks and pilchard seines soon followed, and Rashleigh had a four-gun battery erected on the cliffs to the south for protection during the French wars. One of his most interesting achievements was to obtain a supply of water for his dock basins by building a leat from the Luxulyan Valley. About six miles long, it passes over an aqueduct and through several tunnels, and the cost of its construction and upkeep was met partly by using it to power watermills along the way. The leat can still be seen at the northern end of the Treffry Viaduct (see Walk 12 in *Around the River Fowey*), and is crossed by the Saints' Way just south of Trevanney farm. See also Walk 5 in this book. The population of what was soon renamed Charlestown in honour of its creator had reached nearly 3,000 by 1851. A press advert in 1817 referred to "Charlestown from whence all the china clay raised in Cornwall is shipped", but at first it was mostly the copper mines like Crinnis that kept the port busy, and a foundry was set up in the village mainly in order to supply them with shovels, kibbles, pumps, waterwheels, engines and boilers; as the mines declined the china-clay industry grew, so the foundry turned to supplying equipment for that. As Charlestown Engineering it still flourishes. In 1908 John Lovering built a dry close to the dock, to process liquid clay piped from his pits at Carclaze. The dried clay was stored in the building which now houses the Shipwreck & Heritage Centre; from there a tramway took it to the dockside via the tunnel still clearly visible. The dock was always too small for comfort, and as the ships grew in size so the trade moved to Par and Fowey (and to some extent Pentewan, though that had problems of its own), but coasters of up to 500 tons still use the port, and we were lucky enough to see one come in recently. Liz Luck in *South Cornish Harbours* gives an excellent description of this delicate operation. An occasional visitor is the beautiful brig "Maria Asumpta", built in Spain in 1858 and rebuilt in 1981-2; when she is berthed here she is open for visits at certain hours. For more about the history of this fascinating little port, visit the Shipwreck & Heritage Centre; and I understand that Richard and Bridget Larn are working on a small book about Charlestown to be published soon by the Tor Mark Press.

base of a large pumping-engine house, relics of New Pembroke Mine(*). The path passes through another kissing gate and then over an old wooden stile.

7 Turn left at the road (Biscovey Road), then first right, St Mary's Road. For the rest of the walk, see section 8 in Walk 10.

NEW PEMBROKE MINE

This name was adopted in 1863 when Pembroke Mine, which had during the 1820s been nearly as productive of copper as Crinnis, was reopened. By 1870, New Pembroke had a work-force of about 130, and the engine house whose base still lurks among the vegetation was built about then for a very large (80-inch) pumping engine, which when built by Harveys of Hayle in 1839 had the longest stroke of any engine in Cornwall, twelve feet. This engine provides an example of the way such machinery moved from site to site: she had worked at the Wheal Treasure section of Fowey Consols until 1846 (see Walk 11 in *Around the River Fowey,* though in the first edition I wrongly called the Wheal Treasure engine house Wheal Chance), then went to another of Treffry's mines, Par Consols; she was bought by New Pembroke in 1869, and a few years after the closure of this mine in 1876 she migrated to her last home, a lead mine near Holywell in North Wales. (Like a ship, a Cornish beam engine is always "she", never "it".) Kenneth Brown, who provided me with most of the above information, says, "It is of interest that she was far too big for the needs of New Pembroke so the mine next door (near where the DIY centre now is) prevailed upon the adventurers to run flat-rods from the 80 to drain their shaft - one of very few cases in Cornish mining history where adventurers in one mine paid another to keep their water out!" (Flat-rods were horizontal wooden or occasionally iron rods used to transfer power from an engine or waterwheel to a remote location.)

WALK 10
PAR, ST BLAZEY AND BISCOVEY
with a possible extension to PONTS MILL
Nearly four miles, plus nearly two miles with the extension.

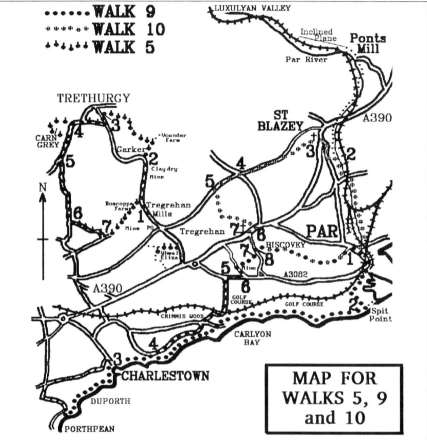

If you share my interest in and admiration for "the King of Mid-Cornwall", J.T.Treffry (or, indeed, if you like exploring railways old and new, or canals and other water engineering works, or old mining areas), this walk will be a "must" for you; if not, you would still, I'm sure, enjoy it for its beauty and variety: an ancient church, country paths and minor roads in delightful wooded valleys and along ridges with wide views, including some of the best panoramic views of the coast on any walk in this book - these are just a few of the pleasures in store. It's quite an easy walk with few if any steep gradients, but you are likely to encounter mud in the valleys near Tregrehan and Ponts Mill, and a stick to deal with vegetation might prove useful on the path above St Blazey church.

The Par Inn (grid reference SX 075536) seems to be the logical start/end point, and I'm told the food there is particularly good, especially Mrs Dingle's pasties. Roadside parking nearby isn't usually hard to find; to drive there from St Austell or Truro, drive east on the A390 and turn right towards Fowey on the A3082. As you approach Par the road passes under two railway bridges close to a big china-clay works, and then the Par Inn is on the left immediately beyond the right turning to Fowey and Par. Several bus and train services link St Austell and Par. A good alternative start/end would be near the St Blazey AFC ground (SX 070547). To drive there, continue along the A390 as far as St Blazey church and turn sharp-right there towards Par. The football ground is a short way along on the left, and there are car parks both beside it and a little further along the road, also on the left. Turn to the end of point 2 in the directions if you are starting there.

1 From the Par Inn walk a few yards along the road almost opposite, signposted to Par and Fowey. You immediately cross a small leat or canalised stream, then the railway line; next comes the Par or Luxulyan River, also canalised, and finally the remains of Treffry's Par Canal (*), now part of a scheme, still progressing in October 1991, to reduce the risk of flooding at Par and St Blazey; some details about the scheme are given on a notice. For the walk, take the track which runs on the left side of this waterway, passing a few houses at first. Soon it becomes a grassy track. Over to the left you have a good view of some of the rather grand brick buildings erected in 1874 as locomotive sheds and engineering works for the Cornwall Minerals Railway but now serving mostly as garages or for storage. This complex includes the UK's only surviving "half-moon" locomotive roundhouse, and is scheduled. The track you are on, formerly the towpath of Treffry's canal, marks the course of the mineral line built in 1855: this is evident from the

---

THE PAR CANAL

Joseph Thomas Austen (1782-1850) took over Fowey Consols mine (on the hill on the east side of Tywardreath Highway) in 1822, and under his control it soon became one of the world's greatest copper mines. The problems involved in transporting the ore to Fowey along the primitive roads prompted him to try a typically daring and imaginative solution: to build a harbour at Par, to get the ore down into the valley a little way south of Ponts Mill by building a tramway on an inclined plane, and to construct a canal linking the two. By the mid-1830s the system was operating. A completely new channel was cut for the Par River, a little to the west of its original course, and the old riverbed was widened and deepened sufficiently to accommodate barges carrying 52 tons of ore, drawn by horses. Three locks, each ninety feet long, were constructed. Later, two more inclined planes from the mine were built, and the canal was extended to Ponts Mill in order to link up with the new tramway Treffry was building through the Luxulyan Valley to serve his quarries and china-clay pits - and eventually, he hoped, to reach his other harbour at Newquay. The business of transferring goods between canal barges and wagons at the foot of the Carmears Incline proved costly in time and labour, and Austen (who in 1838 changed his surname to Treffry, his wife's maiden name - pronounced Tre-fry) planned to replace the canal with a further tramway. In 1855, five years after Treffry's death, this was built; the canal fell out of use, and, to quote the Cornwall Archaeological Unit's report, "There is now little to distinguish the route of the Canal from any other small stream in the area." Its course at the northern end can be traced on the map by following the parish boundary; south of the A390 it ran very close to the canalised river: the new flood-prevention channel is actually the old canal.

row of substantial granite "setts" (sleeper blocks), very similar to those in the Luxulyan Valley (see *Around the River Fowey,* Walk 12). Now the river is close, on the left. Cross the Newquay loop-line with due care and attention. The modern railway line runs on the far side of the river for a little way, then crosses back just before the road at Middleway. (The change in the landscape here over the past two centuries is illustrated by the fact that "A map of Roselyon, dated 1794, shows a stream-work then in operation at Middleway .... with a ship under sail passing close alongside." [A.K.H.Jenkin:*Mines and Miners of Cornwall])* When you reach the road, go left, over the level crossing, and then continue on the riverside path, now called Rundles Walk. On the hillside ahead are the old woods of Prideaux (pronounced "Priddix" in these parts, though not in Padstow), together with newer plantations of conifers at the southern end of the Luxulyan Valley.

2 Nearby on the left now you will see St Blazey church, and the path along the left end of the football pitch makes a convenient short cut to it, so the time has come to decide whether to extend the walk to Ponts Mill, the point where Treffry's canal ended and the mineral line rose by a steep incline to the level of the magnificent viaduct Treffry built in the Luxulyan Valley. (If you do not want to walk there now, turn left beside the pitch and pick up the directions at the end of the section in italics that follows.)

For Ponts Mill (*), continue beside the river. Still running beside it are the Newquay line and the flood-prevention waterway. The large old building with four arched openings is a set of limekilns, though adapted now to other purposes. The wasteland of concrete on the left beside the A390 is the former site of Moon's Aberdeen Laundry, whose stone stack used to be a local landmark. A new residential estate is being built here, called "Aberdeen Close". (I should warn you that from here on, the suggested route is not a right of way; most of it is owned by English China Clays International. I understand from people I have spoken to in Par that it has been a popular walk for many years; ECCI are happy for its unofficial use to continue, but walkers who use it do so on their own responsibility. Particular care must be taken at the Ponts Mill end, where railway lines still in use have to be crossed.) Cross the main road with care and continue on

---

PONTS MILL

By the end of the 12th century, Tywardreath Priory had set up a corn mill here, at a time when this was the lowest bridging point on the Par River (hence the name) and the highest point of navigation. 80-ton vessels could still reach Ponts Mill over 500 years later; but by 1800 the river had brought down vast quantities of silt caused by tin streaming, and when basins for the canal were dug out in 1835 medieval bridges were found 25 feet below the surface. The story of industrial developments at Ponts Mill over the last two centuries, involving hydraulic engineering, tramways and railways, mining, quarrying, china-clay and china-stone processing, forestry and probably much else, is far too complex for me to attempt to tell here. The best account of it I have come across is in *The Luxulyan Valley,* published by the Cornwall Archaeological Unit in 1988. Also good, despite irritating errors like referring to Treffry's great mine as "Fowey Consuls", is John Vaughan's *The Newquay Branch and its Branches* (1991), which includes excellent photographs.

---

the left side of the river. Eventually the path passes under the railway line and then over the river, and you soon realise you are walking along the course of an old two-foot-gauge railway or tramway: see Vaughan page 73 and Plate 114. This linked the Prideaux Wood china-clay kiln to the Cornwall Mineral Railways line, and was probably used only by horse-drawn wagons. Nearby is a sadly battered concrete building labelled "The New Consolidated Mines of Cornwall Ltd" (built about 1920 as a power station for the St Austell Electric Light and Power Company), and sluice gates have been set up to control the water in the river. At this point, cross <u>with due care</u> the railway lines that lead into and beside the china-clay works (the lines may look disused, but see Mr Vaughan's photo No. 115, taken in January 1991), and continue along the narrow road which runs beside a rusty siding and the river. On the right at the point where the siding ends was one of the basins at the terminus of the Par Canal, now choked up and almost unrecognisable. Soon you reach a road which leads left into the china-clay works. The bridge it crosses was built about 1836 to span the diverted river and also the new canal. Above the bridge was another basin where 60-ton canal barges were loaded; in 1991 construction work for the flood prevention scheme was going on here. Notice on the north side of the bridge an iron launder, built to carry back to the river the water from one of the leats in the Luxulyan Valley. If you continue walking in the same line as before and take the left fork in the (muddy) track, you will soon reach a wooden stile and a stone bridge at the foot of the Carmears Incline, with granite setts clear to see. The long climb from here to the site of the Carmears waterwheel is very worthwhile if you have the time and energy for it .... and then, of course, you can tack on Walk 12 from Around the River Fowey! But to complete the walk back to Par, return the same way as far as the St Blazey football ground and turn right towards the church.

At the road turn right *(but see the note in italics which follows)*, and at the A390 cross to St Blazey church (*). If you find it locked you should be able to borrow a key from the Cornish Arms.

NOTE: If you are particularly interested in industrial history, turn left first to see the remains of William West's St Blazey Foundry. The surviving buildings are now used by Smith and Treffry, builders' merchants. West was one of the great engineers, noted particularly for his work at Fowey Consols. He set up this foundry, conveniently close to the canal, in 1848, and for several decades following it was St Blazey's biggest employer. The foundry carried out repair and maintenance work for the mines and built many important beam engines. Five cast-iron road bridges built here in 1873 can still be seen in the Roche area, spanning the Par-Newquay branch line. West died in 1879 and his sons carried on the business for a further fourteen years; after a short period under the ownership of R.Liddicoat & Sons, the foundry closed in about 1900. Kenneth Brown has written about the St Blazey Foundry in the 1991 issue of the Journal of the Trevithick Society, which includes a photograph by him of the curved wall on one side of the entrance, necessary to manoeuvre engine beams and other long loads into the narrow street.

3 Continue the walk by going up Duke Street (beside the church gate) and straight on along the signed footpath. From up here you can get an impression of what this area looked like when the sea lapped up to the churchyard walls: turn the football pitch and recreation ground blue! The

St Blazey

ST BLAZEY AND ITS CHURCH

The old name for the village was Landreath or Landreth, "church-place by the beach"; nearby are Tywardreath, "house upon the beach", and Treesmill, "the mill by the beach". Look where they are on the map: there is no better example in Cornwall, or probably anywhere, of the dramatic effects river-borne detritus can have on a landscape. "That the sea has been driven back from S. Blazey Bridge for at least two miles, within memory, is an indisputable fact," wrote Joseph Polsue (1867); as recently as 1842, Cyrus Redding had written, "the road in one place almost touches upon the head of Tywardreath Bay, by Par Creek, near the church of St Blazey." Saint Blaise, according to legend, disembarked here, but what a 4th-century Armenian bishop would have been doing so far from home is hard to say. Blaise is said to have been tortured to death with a woolcomb and was therefore adopted as the patron saint of weavers and woolcombers; this village has traditionally been associated with the woollen industry, so that seems a more likely explanation of the church's dedication. The church key - an impressive object in itself - can be obtained from the nearby pub. The building, which dates from the 15th century, had a north aisle added in 1839, and was restored in 1897, when the plaster was removed, exposing the attractive silvery granite. There are numerous memorials to members of the Carlyon family (see the note on Tregrehan), but the most prominent and unusual monument commemorates Henry Scobell, "the first Treasurer & Paymaster for ye farm Tyn to Queen Ann". Not buried here but requiring at least a mention is Ralph Allen (1693-1764), the son of a St Blazey innkeeper, who introduced important improvements in the postal service and is said to have earned an average of nearly £12,000 per year for 42 years as a result. He built himself an impressive house near Bath, where he was also involved in quarrying; the Mansion House in Truro is faced with Bath stone which he gave as a wedding present when his niece married Thomas Daniell.

shady, sunken path goes up beside a derelict building. After the gate, where the path was rather overgrown in October 1991, it passes through an area that seems to have been mined. Kenneth Brown suggests that this could be a burrow (waste heap) created by a small trial for tin called Tasman Mine, probably about 1900. Beyond the second gate, keep straight on beside the hedge. The view back on the right from here shows the course of the river and railway up into the Luxulyan Valley, and the scene is dominated by Austen's engine house (Fowey Consols mine): see *Around the River Fowey,* Walk 11. Continue ahead through the farm gate and along the minor road. At the top of the slope is Cornhill Farm, with a good view north across Bodelva Moor (though the flooded pits of the Bodelva china-clay works are not visible from this side of the valley) to Warren Wood and the Prideaux hill fort, below which runs the Saints' Way.

4 At the crossroads go straight on, along the minor road signposted to Tregrehan and St Austell. This brings you down to the attractive wooded valley of Carvear Moor. The small stack and ruined buildings on the right are relics of a dry that belonged to the Carvear china-clay works. The pit which originally supplied clay to it is now part of the Bodelva pit.

5 Take the signed footpath to St Blazey Gate, on the left. This delightful - if at times rather muddy - path runs close to a little stream which flows from the china-clay workings and has deposited sand - a miniature example of the kind of silting which afflicted the Fal, the St Austell River and others in this area. I'm told that this path is known locally as Whitewater Lane. On reaching the edge of the grounds of Tregrehan (*), the path or track curves left, uphill, and gives glimpses of the sea as you approach the main road near Par Parish Church at St Blazey Gate.

6 You reach the main road close to shops and a pub, The Four Lords - whose name probably refers to the four main local landowners, Edgcumbe, Rashleigh, Carlyon and Treffry. (So suggests H.L.Douch, but Canon Hammond in his history of St Austell lists "four lords" as Edgcumbe, Tremayne and two branches of the Sawle family.) Turn right. St Mary's Church, built to the designs of G.E.Street in 1849, is described enthusiastically by Betjeman in his *Shell Guide* to Cornwall. Nikolaus Pevsner wrote (in 1950) of its "pink stone which looks mellow and loveable after 100 years," and thought it "aesthetically more pleasing even than Truro Cathedral." In the churchyard, beside the small door at the south-east end of the church, is "The Biscovey Stone", which probably dates from the 10th century. It was moved here in 1896, having previously served as a gate-post for the toll gate nearby, on the main road. A.G.Langdon, in *Old Cornish Crosses,* complained bitterly of this "illustration of the apathy and want of interest in Cornwall towards its many priceless relics"; his book was published in 1896..... Langdon gives a very full description of this cross shaft, which is beautifully decorated though much eroded, and is inscribed ALRORON ULLICI (or ULCUI?) FILIUS.

7 Turn left opposite the church, down Biscovey Road *(but see the note on Tregrehan for the possibility of extending the walk to there).* The name, meaning house of Covey (or a similar surname), is pronounced "<u>Bis</u>-ca-<u>vay</u>".

8 Take the second turning on the left, St Mary's Road, and then the first right, Hillside Avenue. This becomes a path running between hedges at first,

TREGREHAN

The manor of Tregrehan was part of the property of Henry Bodrugan which passed to the Edgcumbes after the Wars of the Roses: see the note about Bodrugan's Leap, Walk 10. In the 17th century Tregrehan Barton was bought by the Carlyon family, who in the opinion of the historian Hals were probably descended from "Richard Curlyon, alias King Richard I". The present mansion was built in the 18th century and "almost rebuilt within the last twenty years" according to Lake's *Parochial History* (1867). Canon Hammond in his history of St Austell remarks that "The house and grounds are undermined in almost every direction by the workings of Old Crinnis Copper Mine." He could also have mentioned Wheal Eliza and West Par Consols; D.B.Barton mentions that very long levels had to be driven because the Carlyon family banned all shafts and surface workings on their grounds, "save on a penalty of £10,000". Work on laying out the grounds began early last century, and improvements and replantings have continued to the present day. An account written in 1916 said that Tregrehan stood out "above all the Cornish gardens for the richness and health of its conifers"; some of those conifers are now probably the largest specimens of their species in the country. The garden is now also famous for its trees from the southern hemisphere, especially New Zealand, and the camellias planted by Miss Gillian Carlyon during this century. In recent years it has been open to the public on certain days. In 1991 these were Wednesdays, Thursdays and Saturdays from mid-March to the end of June and again in September; please check in the current *Gardens of Cornwall Open Guide.* You could include a visit on this walk, but unfortunately that would involve another half-mile or more on the main road: the entrance is opposite the Stadium (Great Mills etc.), just before the Britannia Inn and the turning to Fowey (A3082). There is a pavement all the way, on the left side of the road. After visiting Tregrehan, if you did decide to walk it, you could reduce the main-road stint by turning right on Pennys Lane and joining the route of Walk 14 a little way into point 6. (The name, by the way, is pronounced "Tregrain", and may mean "wrinkles estate" - work that one out if you can! A.L. Rowse, however, states that it means "hamlet on gravel". For a particularly vivid description of the house and grounds during the late 19th and early 20th centuries, see the last part of Chapter III in *A Cornish Childhood.)*

and then opening up to give wonderful views over St Austell Bay, with the golf links and the main railway line fairly close. Just down the slope below the infants' school is East Crinnis Farm, the site of a very productive copper mine of the same name, which between 1820 and 1841 was controlled by John Taylor: see Walk 5, the note on Polgooth Mine. In the valley, successful tin-streaming enterprises called Sandrycock and Porth, dating back to the mid-18th century, were carried on; interesting details about them are given by A.K. Hamilton Jenkin in *Mines and Miners of Cornwall,* Vol. XIV (pages 19-21). A surfaced track or drive brings you past the impressive buildings of Trenovissick Farm; a short way beyond that, the steaming chimneys of the clay dries at Par come into view; and then you pass among the mobile homes of the Mount Holiday Park. This area was mined by Par Consols (*). On the edge of the "Adventure Playground" is the base of the engine house for a steam whim (winding engine); the base of the stack has, in Kenneth Brown's words, "been turned into a tasteful litter bin!" It's worth walking across the rough ground on the right for the view of Par Harbour (*). On the left near the exit from the Holiday Park is part of another engine house, the impressive bob-wall on which pivoted the beam or bob of Treffry's North 80-inch pumping engine. This is the engine mentioned in the note about New Pembroke Mine, Walk 9. Continue down the road through a bungalow estate, and soon you are back at the Par Inn.

PAR CONSOLS

This group of old mines was reopened about 1834, and like Fowey Consols was controlled by J.T.Treffry until his death in 1850. During the 1840s it was one of the most productive copper mines in Cornwall, employing at least eight steam engines: three for pumping, two for winding, two for stamps - one of which drove a set of a hundred heads - and a small one used to power a sawmill and also to raise and lower skips or wagons on an inclined plane down to Par harbour. In the 1850s tin gradually became the mine's main product, and for a while it was the second biggest tin-producer in the county. A man-engine was installed in 1855, one of the few designed by the St Blazey engineer William West under licence. (For more about man-engines see the note on Tresavean Mine in *A Second View from Carn Marth.*) By the 1860s the mine had as many as fifteen engines at work - and yet the slump in tin prices around 1865 was so bad that the whole operation closed down in 1867. Kenneth Brown informs me that one engine of special interest at Par Consols was a rare 72-inch pumping engine converted by Edward ("Ned") Bull from a two-cylinder Sims combined engine: the cylinder was inverted over the shaft.

PAR HARBOUR

Plans for a harbour at Par were drawn up in 1792. John Smeaton of Eddystone Lighthouse fame, who had designed Charlestown harbour, was involved in producing these plans, and when James Rendell was employed in 1828 by J.T.Austen (Treffry) to design Par harbour, many of Smeaton's suggestions were adopted. Rendell and Austen agreed that it should be built behind the shelter of Spit Point. Soon the two men quarrelled and Austen then took over sole responsibility for the project. Despite great problems caused by wayward currents and shifting sands, by 1830 the work was well advanced, and by the mid-1840s there were not only a southern breakwater 1,200 feet long and an even longer northern wall, together enclosing enough quayside space for over 50 ships, but smelters for tin, copper, silver and lead, a brickworks, facilities for cutting and dressing granite and for handling china clay and china stone, limekilns, ship-repair and ship-building yards, blacksmiths' and carpenters' shops, a flour mill, a pilchard fishery, and even a factory where miners' candles were made. Now, of course, the focus is entirely on china clay, and as a clay port Par is second in importance only to Fowey, which can handle large vessels even at low tide.